WALKING SAFARIS
OF SOUTH AFRICA

Guided walks and trails in
national parks and game reserves

Hlengiwe Magagula and Denis Costello

Published by Struik Travel & Heritage
(an imprint of Penguin Random House South Africa
(Pty) Ltd)
Reg. No. 1953/000441/07
The Estuaries No. 4, Oxbow Crescent,
Century Avenue, Century City, 7441
PO Box 1144, Cape Town, 8000 South Africa

www.penguinrandomhouse.co.za
www.walkingsafarisofsouthafrica.com

First published in 2021
10 9 8 7 6 5 4 3 2 1

Publisher: Pippa Parker
Managing editor: Roelien Theron
Editor: Karen Press
Designer: Gillian Black
Cartographer: Liezel Bohdanowicz
Proofreader: Thea Grobbelaar

Reproduction by Studio Repro
Printed and bound by Novus Print, South Africa

'The blur of hoof and paw' and 'eSwatini's wildest
corner' were first published by *Wild Card*. 'Rhino
tracks and elephant snacks', 'Cooling my feet in
Pafuri', 'Feeling the heat in Limpopo', 'Trailing the
trainee trail guides', 'The pharmacy of the dunes'
and 'Searching for Mabula' were first published by
Wild Card with the support of Trappers. 'Lost spirits
of the lowveld' and 'Barefoot biophilia in Zululand'
were first published by the *Sunday Times*.

Front cover: Hikers take to the wilderness in
anticipation of discovering the secrets of the bush
on a guided dawn walk in Mashatu Game Reserve
(courtesy of Stuart Quinn, Tuli Wilderness; © Emil
von Maltitz)
Half-title page: Elephants in Shamwari Private
Game Reserve browse undisturbed by observing
walkers. (© Ryan Plakonouris)
Contents page: Sightings of rhinos are guaranteed
in Hluhluwe-iMfolozi Park, one of South Africa's most
pristine wilderness areas. (© Isibindi Africa Lodges)
Back cover: Walking safaris in the northern section
of Kruger National Park introduce hikers to a variety
of different habitats. (© Ecotraining)

ACKNOWLEDGEMENTS

Many people from the walking safari sector helped in compiling the information and photographs for
this book. Particular thanks are owed to Duncan Boustead, Bjinse Visser, and Wayne te Brake for
their expert review of particular sections. Thanks to Katherine Kelly and Aine Kelly-Costello for their
helpful comments on an early manuscript, Karen Press for her diligent edit, and the team at Penguin
Random House. Thanks are also due to Todani Moyo for his eloquent foreword. Most of all, I'd like to
give my appreciation to the trail guides who make this wonderful wild activity possible.
Denis Costello

This book would not have been possible without Romi Boom, Magriet Kruger, Sam Lincesso, Peter
Frost, Paul Ash and Elizabeth Sleith, all of whom supported my writing. A special thank you to
the folks who facilitated park visits, including the team at *Wild Card* and SANParks staff Van Rooi
Moreku, Tshepo Mathebula, Vic Mokoena and Fayroush Ludick. I'm grateful to Michelle du Plessis for
explaining the world of trail guide qualifications, and to Markus Jungnickel and walking safari addict
Joe James for contributing their lovely photos.
Hlengiwe Magagula

CONTENTS

FOREWORD

I first fully recognised the power of the wilderness narrative in Anchorage, Alaska, at the 8th World Wilderness Congress in 2005. I watched Dr Ian Player hold a collective audience of some 1,200 people spellbound: US politicians, conservationists, Alaskan fishermen and lumberjacks, shamans, Inuits and Native American chiefs. You could literally hear a pin drop as the audience sat mesmerised by his stories of the African wilderness. It touched me deeply, as it did the entire assembly of listeners, who honoured the great storyteller with a standing ovation.

I am humbled by the fact that I can consider myself to have been a close personal friend of the late Ian Player. Over the years of our friendship I was able to witness first-hand the passion that this iconic conservationist had for people to spend time in southern Africa's wilderness areas – even if only for a short while. It was impossible not to be influenced by the sheer force of 'Madolo's' immovable belief in the power of wilderness to unlock a fundamental need, shared by all humans, to connect with their essential nature, their true being. This led to the founding of the Wilderness Leadership School, which through its primitive trails continues to inculcate *hlonipe* (respect) for wild spaces and cultural integrity through a direct experience of nature.

Ian Player and others felt intuitively that an immersion in nature can bring about a shift in consciousness, and that, by exposing more people of all ages and from all cultures to this harmonising experience, changes could be brought about on other levels too. They sought to make all trailists ambassadors for the preservation of the planet and, in particular, the wilderness.

We know today that the vision of Ian Player and his friend and mentor Magqubu Ntombela pre-dates the science now available that shows the immense value that connecting to wild spaces has for humans. Not only does it facilitate mental and physical well-being, it also arouses a sense of sheer joy and awe for a place that may in short order feel more like home than home. As wild natural spaces across the globe diminish in extent, there is a growing realisation that the very protection of this vital component of planetary wellness is critical to the future of human wellness and, indeed, humankind.

While science races ahead to provide paradigms for meaningful mitigations against the major threats of climate change, loss of biodiversity and zoonotic diseases, and the right of all people to clean water and air, the politics will be changed by the will of people intent on choosing to live purposeful lives that encompass behavioural, social and environmental change.

Kwandwe Private Game Reserve

Traversing South Africa's wilderness areas on foot is not just enriching and enjoyable, it also reinforces the need to conserve the country's remaining wild places.

Great adventures in wild places have long been the stuff of stories told by all cultures. Perhaps it is time to rekindle the desire for similar adventures; to satisfy the deepest yearnings of our wilder sides; to put aside, for a while, our technological devices and the difficulties of our current times; to make time to just 'be' in places that excite our very being.

Ian Player was perhaps the larger-than-life subject of many a tale, the man who rode horseback through the wilds of the Hluhluwe-iMfolozi Park, who worked tirelessly to protect the southern white rhino, and who fought to protect sensitive areas from mining. However, he would bow to the thrill of the Zulu storyteller who brought to life the traditional stories of the elders, painting a verbal picture of the sacred hunting grounds of King Shaka where vast herds of wildebeest and elephants and prides of lions roamed; of the use of traditional medicine through the ages; and of weather phenomena that foretold the fate of the crops.

Perhaps it is time to create new experiences. If we don't use this time to create our own adventures, what stories will we be telling future generations?

Todani Moyo
Chairman: Wilderness Foundation Global
www.wildernessfoundationglobal.org

Limpopo

Makuleke
Contractual Park

Luvuhu

Kruger
National Park

MOZAMBIQUE

Letaba Ranch
Nature Reserve

Groot Letaba

Olifants (Lepelle)

Klaserie Private
Nature Reserve

Timbavati

Timbavati Private
Nature Reserve

Manyeleti Private
Nature Reserve

SOUTH
AFRICA Sabie

Mbombela
(Nelspruit)

Crocodile (Umgwenya)

Komatipoort

INSET: KRUGER NATIONAL PARK AND
GREATER KRUGER AREA

TRAIL TYPES

Day walks

Wilderness trails

Backpacking trails

Nossob

Kgalagadi
Transfrontier
Park

Molopo

Kuruman

Kurun

N10 Upington N14

R64

NAMIBIA

Orange

N7 N14

N10

Orange

N12

NORTHERN CAPE

Springbok

SOUTH AFRICA

Loxton

Great Karoo

ATLANTIC

OCEAN

Doring

Cederberg

Sutherland

Beaufort
West

WESTERN
CAPE

Laingsburg

N9

Saldanha

Worcester

Klein

Karoo

Gondwana
Game Reserve

Cape Town N1

Montagu

Sanbona
Wildlife Reserve

George

Mossel
Bay

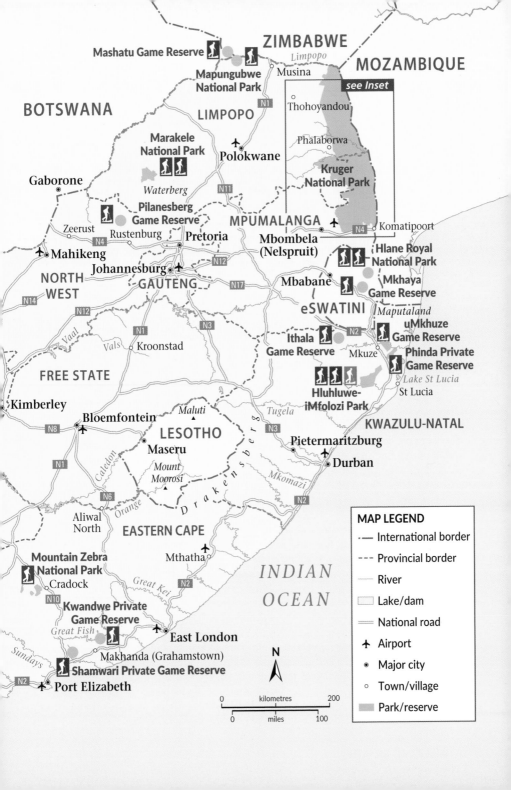

INTRODUCTION

Denis Costello

Taking to the wild on foot means that walkers can enjoy vistas not easily accessed on a driving safari – such as this spectacular view from Salpeterkop in the Mountain Zebra National Park.

A braid of animal tracks threads through themeda grass to a shallow pan, where rhino wallow. A baobab tree shades a rocky outcrop, a leopard lookout. In the void of a sandstone gorge, martial eagles glide, effortless in the updraft. And through it all we wander, experiencing Africa's bushveld just as our ancestors did – on foot.

The great conservationist Dr Ian Player, who more than anyone made it possible for us to experience South Africa's wild places safely on foot, said how important it was for people 'to feel the soul of Africa through the soles of their feet'. And Africa's soul is in its wilderness, away from the tracks of vehicles. In South Africa's many wildlife reserves, safaris are usually a motorised activity and the regular notices to 'Please Stay in Your Vehicle' are sound advice. After all, these wild areas are the preserve of big cats, elephant, buffalo, hippo, rhino, crocodile and other potential dangers. And yet, we wish it were otherwise. For most of human history, our forebears have walked these open spaces, and that yearning to wander freely on foot in the wild still lingers in everyone.

Happily, we can still do so. South Africa has a unique set of characteristics that makes it the world centre of walking safaris in big game areas: a huge expanse of protected habitat with healthy populations of wildlife in well-managed reserves; high-quality tourism infrastructure with trail guides of the highest calibre; and a climate and culture that favour outdoor adventure. Each year, South African national parks and private reserves welcome tens of thousands of walking safari visitors who can avail themselves of a growing number of wonderful opportunities to explore the wilds on foot.

The first question that arises is an obvious one – is it safe? The answer is simple: yes, when we observe the rules, as instructed by professional guides, it is very safe. The next question follows – isn't it easier to view wildlife from a vehicle? That is true, but it's not an either/or choice, as there's always an opportunity to do both. Being on foot is a different experience to driving through a reserve. Which leads to another question – why do it? And that is even easier to answer, for so many reasons.

On a motor safari we are observers of the natural world, and on a foot safari we are participants in it. For nature lovers, no experience is better than being on a trail at dawn, listening to the chorus of birdsong, knowing not what wonders await. From the grassy dunes of the Kalahari to the heathlands of the Cape and subtropical forest of the lowveld, South Africa has an exceptional variety of walking terrains, many teeming with wildlife. Vast wilderness areas are conserved where little has changed since earth's earliest humans first roamed them. It's a rare and special thing to walk this land, where we are but one animal among many.

Exploring on foot adds excitement as we must stay alert, watching and listening for what could be ahead. Approaching big animals closely on foot is not the goal, but it happens, and when it does, it makes the heart beat faster. Animals react differently to pedestrians. When we're in a vehicle, they don't really regard us with much interest, but when we're on foot it's another matter. There is no mistaking the eye contact of an elephant, buffalo or lion that sees a person as a potential threat or meal.

A dawn walk will enrich any safari. It's a chance to get close to nature's smaller treasures: burrows and nests, insects and birds, animal tracks and droppings, seed pods and flowers. Examine where an elephant has worn a tree smooth. Inspect an aardvark's burrow or a rhino's midden. Inhale the scents of sweet thorn blossom. It's

Denis Costello

The golden light of early morning, resplendent in the Kgalagadi Transfrontier Park, is one of the many rewards of a dawn walk.

Denis Costello

Trail guides are master interpreters of the signs and secrets of the bush.

Denis Costello

interesting and educational. Trail guides are knowledgeable, and enjoy sharing their love for the bushveld. The experience is much less about covering ground than about being in the wild on foot, using all our senses to appreciate the wonders of the natural world.

Multi-day walking safaris are a deeper dive. Going off-grid on a wilderness trail or backpacking trail means overnighting deep in the bushveld, immersed in nature, enjoying the calm that remoteness brings. It's an antidote to our touchscreen addictions, forcing us to interact with the tangible world. To enjoy the peace of walking in silence or stopping for an hour or two to do absolutely nothing but sit, admire and absorb is deeply therapeutic.

Apart from the personal benefits it offers, walking is also good for conservation. As an activity, it is low-impact and sustainable, giving visitors access to pristine nature zones with a minimal ecological footprint. The very existence of walking safaris is grounded in the desire to give visitors a deeper understanding of park ecosystems and create new, lifelong ambassadors for conservation.

FIRST STEPS

One day, a woman walked barefoot in wet sand on a dune. Over hours and days, wind filled her footprints with dry sand and crushed seashells, which over centuries hardened and preserved their shape. For millennia, the whims of geography and climate buried the prints nine metres deep and then exposed them again. In 1995, 117,000 years after the woman's shoreline stroll, three of her prints were found. The site is at Langebaan Lagoon in the West Coast National Park, about 100 kilometres north-west of Cape Town, and the marks are known as Eve's Footprint – the earliest preserved human footprints on the planet.

Joe James

A hiker on the Kruger Park's Napi Wilderness Trail ponders the end of another day in the bush.

Homo sapiens had walked in Africa for at least 100,000 years before those prints were formed. In recent years the science of DNA has revolutionised the study of the spread of our species. In 2019, *Nature* magazine published the work of a group of researchers who had used analyses of mitochondrial DNA to pinpoint our direct ancestors living in an area south of the Zambezi River basin in what is now Botswana, around 200,000 years ago. Yes, we have been walking in southern Africa for a very long time indeed, and it's conceivable that 'Eve' is in everyone's family tree.

For most of history, she and other humans were merely one animal species among many moving on foot in the veld; they were not at the top of the food chain. They gradually learned to find safety in numbers, and use their superior social and communication skills and dexterous tool-making hands to gain the advantage over even the biggest game. With the advent of settlement and agriculture, new battle lines with nature were drawn – fences of thorn, ramparts of earth, walls of stone. Fire, once used on a small scale by hunter-gatherers to flush out prey, was deployed to transform landscapes for farming. Eventually we favoured and domesticated some animals, to the point where today 60 per cent of all mammals on earth are poultry, sheep and cattle.

On much of the planet, the pressure on the natural world was unbearable. Habitats were obliterated, species pushed to extinction. Happily for us present-day hominins, much of sub-Saharan Africa took a different path, and thousands of years after settled farming had taken hold in the Middle East's 'fertile crescent', nomadic hunter-herding was still the norm. Today, the San people of Botswana are direct descendants of those first humans, and a small number still hunt as barefoot as 'Eve'.

When change came in southern Africa, it was sudden in evolutionary terms. From AD 500, the arrival of Bantu-speaking peoples from the north brought with it farming and cattle-herding. The modern history of South Africa is a story of settlement, expansion and

Elephants cross the dry riverbed of the Motloutse in Mashatu Game Reserve in Botswana.

fences. Guns transformed hunting. The landscape changed forever, and wilderness areas were coveted for cattle, mining and plantations, with traditional landowners dispossessed. And yet, much did not change. Conditions in marginal areas were hostile to farming and fencing: too arid, too hot, or infested with malaria and tsetse fly. Today, those who walk away from the vehicle tracks in the Kgalagadi Transfrontier Park or Kruger National Park find themselves in a wilderness little disturbed by humans.

For many southern Africans, the bushveld is in their blood. Some have inherited the bush skills honed by their ancestors over millennia, while a tiny few still live a semi-nomadic life. Historically, walking with wildlife was nothing unusual for rural dwellers. As late as the 1920s, visitors to the Kruger National Park were happy to explore the terrain on foot and camp wild without escorts. Then, as numbers grew, safety became a concern and park visitors were confined to cars. The country urbanised, and many would spend their entire lives without encountering a wild animal. It took a few decades, and the work of visionary individuals, before we could once again walk wild in South Africa's national parks and reserves.

The concept of recreational walking safaris is very new. For almost all of history, walking in the wilderness was strictly a matter of business – hunting, or searching for new lands to cultivate, roads to build, ores to extract. It was hunters who first saw the need to protect the land if any game was to survive: 'conservation' originally meant conservation for future hunting. It may have been for selfish reasons, but the consequences of this shift in attitude were good. Starting with the proclamation of the Hluhluwe and iMfolozi game reserves in 1895 and the Sabie Game Reserve (now part of the Kruger National Park) in 1898, South Africa took the lead in Africa in setting aside areas where hunting was restricted.

Today, there are two ways to look at the status of wildlife habitat conservation in South Africa. On the one hand, it is a story of decimation. As in other parts of the world, human activities have squeezed nature, hunted species to extinction, dammed rivers and gobbled up enormous areas of wilderness for farming and mining. Big game is no longer free to roam its natural range and is confined to fenced reserves. And yes, all the reserves in South Africa are fenced.

On the other hand, it can be argued that the worst has passed. Over 100,000 square kilometres or 8 per cent of the country's terrestrial area is conserved, in a 60/40 split of private and state ownership. This is quite an achievement, given the competing pressures for land use. There is a substantial lobby that recognises the value of protecting areas of conservation from extractive industries and other destructive uses, and the state is committed to the promotion of tourism in a sustainable way. Some parks have long-term plans to expand, and large transfrontier parks are slowly being established in partnership with neighbouring countries. There are ongoing land claims in state-owned areas of conservation, but it is reassuring that in cases where claims have been settled, there are proven economic models whereby the owners can use the land for their own benefit while maintaining its conservation status. A good example is the Makuleke Contractual Park (also known as the Pafuri Triangle) in the north of the Kruger National Park (see chapter 5), which is a superb walking destination.

Conservationist Norman Carr is regarded as the father of the walking safari; he began taking visitors on foot into South Luangwa National Park in present-day Zambia in the mid-1950s. At a time when a safari was synonymous with hunting, Carr led the way in showing that wildlife tourism could be a driver for conservation, and could also support local communities. In South Africa, another visionary leader, Ian Player, began organising wilderness trails in KwaZulu-Natal at the end of the 1950s. While working as a ranger for the Natal Parks Board (now Ezemvelo KZN Wildlife), Dr Player became convinced that inviting visitors to participate in a genuine wilderness experience was essential to habitat conservation. It was a challenge to convince the Board of the viability of letting people explore the parks on foot, but once given permission, he and his friend Magqubu Ntombela – a game guard descended from a long line of Zulu warriors in the area between Hluhluwe and iMfolozi – took more than 3,000 walkers into the wilderness areas of iMfolozi and Lake St Lucia game reserves. On leaving the Natal Parks Board to start the Wilderness Leadership School (see chapter 1), Dr Player said, 'I felt compelled to make it possible for more people to have wilderness experiences so that their lives could be changed, and then they too would become advocates for the fast diminishing wilderness and the parks.'

It took some time for the trails concept to be adopted in the Kruger National Park. The idea of running overnight wilderness trails in the park was mooted in 1968, but it was not until 1978 that the first trail, Wolhuter Wilderness Trail, was established by Regional Ranger Mike English. As well as observing the success of Dr Player's wilderness trails, English had first-hand experience of trails operating since the late 1960s in Gonarezhou National Park in Zimbabwe, close to the Kruger Park. Day walks from rest camps followed in the early 1990s.

Joe James

A herd of elephants makes an appearance on the Wolhuter Wilderness Trail, the first such trail to be established in the Kruger National Park.

The costs of running national parks are enormous, especially given the need for anti-poaching measures such as better fencing and aerial patrols that have grown more urgent in recent years. The parks therefore come under pressure to generate more revenue through increased commercialisation – more private concessions in the parks, more roads, more cultural and sporting event permits. To their credit, they have been largely successful in resisting this pressure, and have focused on finding ways to increase visitor numbers without allowing more infrastructure to encroach on wilderness areas. Bushwalking activities are a good fit with this strategy.

Beyond the national parks, an increasing number of private reserves in South Africa are offering walking safaris, having recognised the growth in demand for eco-friendly tourism and active recreation. Visitors are essential to the protection of wilderness areas, their money financing defence against destructive uses and providing income to rural communities. For everyone who loves the African wilderness, the threat of climate change and loss of biodiversity can sometimes feel overwhelming. By choosing to appreciate it on foot, we can make a small contribution to conserving what is left for the next generation.

BIG 5, SMALL 5

This book is about walks that are guided in areas with potentially dangerous animals – we use the term 'big game' for these species. While 'game' may evoke connotations of the hunting world, its meaning has evolved such that the term 'game-viewing' encompasses the appreciation of all sorts of wildlife in its natural setting. In our context, big game refers to animals that could be harmful if approached by untrained people, including elephant, rhino, buffalo, hippo, giraffe, hyena and big cats. All of the walks in this book require escort by specialist trail guides, who are usually armed.

Mike Dexter

Trail guides like Eric Maripane are adept at spotting the telltale signs of animals in the vicinity.

Walking is the best way to appreciate all nature has to offer, from conspicuous big game to a multitude of smaller and sometimes overlooked species.

Large blue charaxes

Dropwing dragonfly

Dwarf mongoose

Leopard tortoise

Female trapdoor spider

Puff adder

Southern African python with its shedded skin

Inspecting dung for signs of dung beetle activity

A close-up view of the larvae of a cherry spot moth.

The teeth of a buffalo tell a tale.

We prefer 'big game' to the alternative term 'big 5', which was originally a hunter's brag list that has morphed into a marketing term used by reserves to denote elephant, buffalo, lion, leopard and rhino. While it's possible to meet all of these animals on a walk, they are not the main focus of the experience, and guides like to tease 'big 5' fanatics with a tongue-in-cheek 'small 5' list – the elephant shrew, buffalo weaver, antlion, leopard tortoise and rhino beetle. In any case, the selected big five species is a rather arbitrary anachronism. Who wouldn't be happy with a day when they spotted just a cheetah or a pack of African wild dogs? And one of the greatest parks in Africa has only two of the big five (a clue – it's too arid for large animals).

Within this lies the truth about walking safaris. Their purpose is not to look for big animals, although these will be encountered. Instead, the door is opened to the wide, wonderful world of nature that can only be appreciated on foot. It's not hiking, and is a different experience to self-guided walking in South Africa's many other fabulous parks. There are no marked trails, and it's rare to see another human footprint. There are no benches for rest, no railings at the cliff-top lookout. Far from the whiff of diesel and hot asphalt, walkers are embraced by the reassuring ambience of nature. That's why the descriptions of walks in this guide give only vague indications of routes and timings. Each one is an exploration, a slow journey of serendipity.

Taking time to stop on a trail offers a chance to examine tracks (above left) and scat (above right).

WHERE TO WALK WITH WILDLIFE

Walking safaris take place in areas where wildlife roams free, and guides are compulsory because of the presence of potentially dangerous big game. Not surprisingly, most walking safaris are therefore found where the big animals live: the lowveld areas of woodland and moist savannah habitats in three of South Africa's nine provinces, namely northern KwaZulu-Natal, eastern Mpumalanga and eastern Limpopo. There are also good walking options to be found away from the lowveld, where reserves have the advantage of being malaria-free but have less tourism infrastructure and provide fewer accommodation choices. Walks in the borderland parks and reserves on the fringes of the Kalahari offer a contrast in landscapes and wildlife, while those in the Western and Eastern Cape have lower numbers of game but compensate with stunning landscapes and beautiful flora.

Parks and reserves are in either state, community or private ownership, and state reserves may be owned nationally or by provincial governments, with national ownership providing the strongest legal protection against changes to their conservation status. In this guide we use the term 'reserve' to refer to all of these types. Land ownership and use in South Africa is a complex topic, with competing pressures from conservation, tourism, hunting, farming and mining interests, and there are many ongoing legal claims by communities to have land returned that was taken from them under apartheid-era legislation.

The protected areas in public ownership are operated by a plethora of agencies, the largest of which are SANParks and Ezemvelo KZN Wildlife. Ezemvelo owns and manages the parks in KwaZulu-Natal, while SANParks operates in all the other provinces and works with neighbouring countries to manage five transfrontier parks. The state agencies not only own the parks, but also operate a great number of rest camps and resorts in them and have a mandate to make them accessible to all. Unlike East African safari destinations,

EcoTraining

Walkers skirt a buffalo herd in Kruger National Park, the reserve with the widest range of walking safaris in South Africa.

Mapungubwe National Park is studded with magnificent baobab trees.

Denis Costello

public parks in South Africa allow self-driving and provide affordable accommodation. This means that most South African walking safaris are not confined to the luxury market.

Outside the publicly owned parks, private reserves operate a spectrum of activities including game-viewing, research, hunting, game farming and wildlife breeding for profit. Most play an important role in habitat and wildlife conservation, rewilding former farmland and reintroducing locally extinct species. A handful are guilty of unethical predator breeding for petting and selfies. In the Greater Kruger reserves, where private lands abut the state-owned Kruger National Park, fences have been removed and this benefits wildlife and enriches the visitor experience.

All this adds up to a complicated web of choices when it comes to planning and booking walking safaris, and this guide is designed to help visitors decide where to go. Twenty-one reserves meet our criteria as guided walking safari destinations. They include a few reserves beyond South Africa's borders which are easy for South African residents and visitors to access. These are the places where guiding is compulsory, for safety reasons. This guide does not cover the self-guided walks that can be experienced in other parks and reserves around South Africa.

Walking safari destinations are found throughout South Africa, with the best options in the areas that combine large game populations and good tourism infrastructure: Hluhluwe-iMfolozi Park in KwaZulu-Natal and the Kruger National Park and its adjacent 'Greater Kruger' reserves that span the east of Mpumalanga and Limpopo provinces. For international visitors, these are the easiest areas to access, having the best flight connections. They also have private walk operators that can make the arrangements for non-self-drive visitors. Away from these zones, tour options are fewer and the most practical way to access the reserves is to self-drive.

The Kruger National Park has the highest volume of walkers, with about 5,000 annually going on SANParks wilderness and backpacking trails, and many more going on day walks and private trails. In this park the main concern for visitors is getting a place on a trail. In other parks, walks are sometimes restricted due to low numbers of bookings, or lack of availability of trail staff. Booking a walk in advance is essential in those parks to avoid disappointment.

TYPES OF WALKS

Walking safaris fall into three categories: day walks from camps, lodges and park gates; multi-day wilderness trails from dedicated trail camps; and backpacking trails. The reserves that host walking safaris are shown on the map (see pages 6–7).

This book concentrates on walks which are offered as the main activity of the day, as an alternative to a game drive. There's a wonderful selection spanning geography and comfort levels, cost and difficulty. There's genuinely something for everyone.

Occasionally it's possible to get a little taste of bushwalking before setting out on the real thing. Some fenced camps have self-guided perimeter trails, which are a perfect way to wind down at the end of the day – or even to explore after dark. Surprises can appear on the other side of the fence. Examples in the Kruger National Park include the Rhino Trail in Berg-en-Dal Rest Camp, Punda Maria's Flycatcher Trail and the Biyamiti Camp trail.

Day walks

The staple of walking safaris is the dawn walk. With animals hungry and on the move, cooler conditions, and the low-angled light favoured by photographers, this is the ideal time to be out in the veld. As the birds begin their pre-dawn song, walkers gather around steaming cups of coffee and fresh rusks in anticipation of the day's adventure. Walkers are usually taken to the starting point in a game-viewing vehicle, with everyone wrapped against the chill of dawn.

Encountering big game on foot is an exciting part of the trails experience.

Walks can vary in intensity. Some are just an amble for a couple of kilometres lasting about an hour, while others can last four hours or more and cover a lot of ground. A handful of day walks described in this guide have a goal – examples are cheetah tracking in Mountain Zebra National Park and black rhino tracking in Phinda Private Game Reserve – but typically walks don't have names, distances or fixed routes. When chatting about their day, guides refer to local place names for *spruits* (streams) and *koppies* (hills), or to their favourite trees.

As the day warms up, wildlife activity slows down. While every bush walk is potentially a good one, walks in the middle of the day are not likely to be as rewarding as those earlier on – and so this time might be better spent enjoying a siesta or cooling off in the camp pool. Then, as the sun drops, animals are on the move again. Afternoon walks tend to be shorter than the morning ones and, if it's hot, a drive might be preferable. The early evening light is good for photos, and the 'blue hour' after sunset is when many sightings of crepuscular animals such as hyena and porcupine occur.

Wilderness trails

To take the walking experience a step further, there's a multitude of overnight bush walks where guests stay at a dedicated trail camp. These are more intensive and immersive than day walks, off-grid and away from other visitors, and are highly recommended as the best way to enjoy walking safaris. Group sizes are small – a maximum of eight people – and often the trails are seasonal, suspended during the summer heat or winter chill. Full catering is the norm, and three nights is the most popular duration. For vegans, vegetarians and others with particular dietary needs, it's best to contact the walk operator in advance to discuss your requirements.

Overnight trail camps span a wide range of comfort standards, from sleeping on a ground mat to extremely luxurious tents with en-suite facilities. There is almost endless variety, as walking safari operators keep innovating. While the common denominator is escape into the bushveld to spend time on foot, a variety of terms is used throughout this guide for

A campfire sets the scene for an evening of storytelling on the Wolhuter Wilderness Trail in the Kruger National Park.

these trails and their camps, including trail camp, walking safari, wilderness trail and explorer camp. Walks from trail camps tend to be longer than day walks from other camps and lodges. The main walk takes place at dawn, followed by a mid-morning brunch. In the afternoon there's typically a drive, which may incorporate a short walk and a sundowner drink. Evenings are spent swapping stories by a campfire, and bedtime is early.

Trail camps have minimal fencing, or none at all. Some are fixed and have permanent structures, such as the SANParks wilderness trails in the Kruger National Park. Others are temporary 'fly camps' that are erected at the start of each walking season and returned to nature at the end, like Ezemvelo's wilderness trails, the Pioneer Trail in Gondwana Game Reserve, and Pafuri Walking Safaris. Some wilderness trails, such as those operated by the Lowveld Trail Company and Tanda Tula in Timbavati Reserve, see bespoke fly camps freshly set for each booking.

Other wilderness trails are mobile, slackpacking style, where the camp magically appears at a new location each day. Examples are Africa on Foot's Wilderness Trail and some trails offered by Spirited Adventures. Other trails mix more than one type of experience, with a combination of fixed and wild camping. One night can be spent under the stars, and the next in a comfortable tent with a shower outside the door. The Luvuvhu Discovery Trail offered by Pafuri Walking Safaris, Ezemvelo's Hluhluwe-iMfolozi Explorer Trail and WalkMashatu fall into this category.

TRAILS OF THE MIND

The word 'trail' appears many times in this book, but it might not mean what you think it does.

If you hiked the mighty Appalachian Trail, enjoyed the stunning Otter Trail, or survived a mystical Inca Trail, you followed a well-mapped path in the footsteps of many before you.

But sometimes a trail is not a trail. In the world of walking safaris, the only trails encountered are the transient tracks created by animals. When you hear 'wilderness trail', it's better to think of it as a wilderness experience on foot. There are no routes as such, other than those in the minds of the guides. So, don't expect to see any route maps here, or hour-by-hour descriptions of where you will go. And forget about finding any artificial steps, bridges or trail markers. Instead, get ready for a wilderness adventure.

Backpacking trails

The toughest multi-day trails have walkers carrying everything they need in backpacks for 'leave no trace' expeditions. These are offered in the Kruger National Park and Greater Kruger reserves, and in Hluhluwe-iMfolozi Park. Sometimes hikers even sleep without tents, taking turns to keep watch through the night, and this style is usually referred to as a 'primitive trail'. The most extreme walking safari has adventurers traversing the entire length of the Kruger National Park over several visits, meandering some 600 kilometres through the wilderness.

Denis Costello

'Packing light' is the byword for hikers on backpacking trails, such as the Primitive Trail in Hluhluwe-iMfolozi Park, which require participants to carry everything they need.

Phinda Private Game Reserve is one of several private reserves that offer their guests a walking safari experience.

andBeyond.com

CHOOSING A WALKING SAFARI OPERATOR

Most of the walks in this guide are operated directly by the big state agencies, SANParks and Ezemvelo KZN Wildlife. SANParks licenses private concessions within some of its parks, several of which offer walks, and these are also included. Outside the state-owned parks, some private reserves promote walking safaris, especially in the Greater Kruger area and in the Western and Eastern Cape. Any walking safari is a marvellous experience, and once on the trail there are no great differences between public and private operators. As for lodges or trail camps, there is something for every pocket.

In most parks the only walking options are those provided by the park operator, but in a few there are choices to be made. In general, private lodges and camps are more luxurious and more expensive than state-owned ones. With a few exceptions, they operate on an 'all-inclusive' basis for walking activities. As well as targeting higher spenders, the private reserves and the concessions within state parks excel in marketing and internet search engine optimisation, so they soak up a lot of the international visitor sector. This suits domestic visitors just fine. It maximises revenue from inbound tourism, while leaving space at publicly owned camps for the self-drive, self-catering mode preferred by many South Africans. It's feasible to combine both public and private venues on one trip, but it's not possible to stay at one and walk at the other on the same day, as walks usually start early.

While private lodges and camps provide a higher degree of luxury than those in state ownership, when it comes to the actual walking, the experience is similar. SANParks, Ezemvelo and private guides are all well trained and have a deep knowledge of natural history. Private operations can afford to pay for the highest-qualified guides, but there are many excellent guides working for the national parks too.

Apart from price and comfort, the main difference between public and private walk operations is their degree of flexibility. Walks operated by SANParks and Ezemvelo are rigid in format: multi-day trails depart on particular days for fixed durations, and walkers must fit in with the calendar. Private operators of wilderness trails can offer bespoke arrangements in terms of number of nights, and can tune the timing and duration of walks to suit their guests. They can operate one-off trails with specialist guides and even offer up to a week of slackpacking that blends fly-camping at temporary sites, fixed camps and lodges. High-end lodges generally have a maximum of six walkers on a trail, but they can also cater for smaller walking parties and go out with just one or two guests. At this end of the market it's common for all lodge guides to have a trails qualification, and this means that

Trail guides Calvin de la Rey (left) and Kobus Strauss (right) discuss the role of trees in the Kruger National Park's Pafuri area.

impromptu bush walks are possible during game drives.

When booking at private lodges it's important to check whether walking will definitely be available. Usually, trail walking requires the allocation of two guides, whereas game drives can take place with one. It can happen that because of the staffing requirement, and the need to cater for all guests, trail walking at some lodges is an 'all or none' activity. In other words, if there are eight guests at a lodge, and just one does not want to walk, then a drive will take place instead.

If walking is to be a key element of your safari, beware of lodges that say it is an option when it is not their focus. At some venues, walks are offered only after the morning drives are finished; these are best avoided in favour of a lodge where walking is available as the main activity of the day.

Another factor to consider when choosing to patronise a private reserve is the availability of trophy hunting. There are over 1,000 private reserves in South Africa and most of them derive some income from hunting, especially in areas that are not popular for photographic tourism. Mainstream hunting is not controversial, and indeed many trail guides and walkers hunt. Game management, which can include transfers and culling, occurs in all reserves, state and private. But the money that can be made from hunting trophy animals has led to abominable practices, including the 'canned hunting' of captive-bred big cats, baiting, and the legal trophy hunting of vulnerable species including elephant, lion, leopard and rhino.

Trophy hunting is especially controversial in some of the private and community-owned Greater Kruger reserves that share unfenced boundaries with the Kruger National Park. Occasionally a hunting incident erupts into the news and visitors are shocked to discover that it goes on, as they think they are 'in the Kruger' and would certainly not have been enlightened by the reserve websites, which don't mention hunting. It's important to note that private reserves in Greater Kruger are not under single ownership, but are run by collectives of owners who share traversing rights for game-viewing (but not traversing rights for hunting). Owners and concession holders may be vehemently opposed to trophy hunting, and yet unable to prevent their neighbours from welcoming those who kill for fun. By supporting lodges and walk operators that focus solely on photographic tourism, visitors can encourage a shift in business practices and the elimination of trophy hunting.

Overseas visitors will discover that South Africans have a rich vocabulary to describe the natural environment and their love of being there. While English may be the lingua franca of tourism, many a guide's language is enriched by words borrowed from other languages, especially Afrikaans.

LEXICON OF THE LAND

One all-encompassing Dutch word conjures up the wild African expanses: *veld*. In German and Anglo-Saxon (Old English), it is *feld*, becoming 'field' in English. 'Veld' refers to any uncultivated land where animals and happy hikers roam free.

A small army of descriptive qualifiers tells us more about the varieties of veld. *Bushveld* describes vast swathes of subtropical southern Africa and encompasses scrublands, thickets, woodlands, or any combination of these. *Scrubveld* is a synonym for 'bushveld', and *karooveld* refers to the stunted vegetation of the arid lands of the Karoo region.

At altitude – most of the country – the land is referred to as *highveld*. Much of it is flat, with poor soils, a landscape of *grassveld* supporting a low density of wildlife. Below 1,200 metres, it drops to *middleveld* and then to *lowveld* – the areas below 600 metres near Mozambique, from the Limpopo River south through the Kingdom of eSwatini to Maputaland and the Indian Ocean. At any height, *backveld* is remote and unsophisticated country.

Thornveld refers to the drier areas where acacias and other thorny trees predominate. Lands that are even more arid are *sandveld* – poor grazing with dry, sandy soil. Where conditions are good, there is nutritious grassland called *sweetveld*. On the other hand, a *sourveld* or *suurveld* area supports less game because it has coarse grass containing compounds that make it unpalatable. A particular biome unique to the Western Cape is *fynbos* ('fine bush'), heathland dominated by heathers, proteas and restios.

HILLS AND VALES

Out in the veld, a *koppie* is a little rocky hill, much loved by leopards, dassies and walkers looking for a view. Something bigger, a prominent peak, is a *kop*, Afrikaans for 'head', and a *krans* or crown is a sheer face or precipice. Compounding these words we get *kranskop* and *kranskoppie*, or a hill with a sheer face. A *rand* is a ridge and *randjie* is the diminutive form, while a *berg* is a proper mountain. *Berg*, *rand*, *kop* and *krans* make an appearance in numerous place names, as does *draai*, a bend or curve. Cutting into a *berg*, a cleft or ravine is a *kloof* and a bigger gap or pass is a *poort*.

Trail walkers perch on a koppie in Kruger National Park.

Denis Costello

WATER WORDS

Nothing will survive long in the veld without water, and its availability and distribution determine where we and the wildlife roam. As many waterways are ephemeral, the term *drainage line* is often used in place of 'river' or 'stream', to reduce disappointment. And despite its liquid sound, a *spruit* is a little stream that may be more often dry than wet. The isiZulu and isiXhosa word *donga* describes a dry gully created by water erosion, especially one with steep sides. When water levels in a river are high, it's wise to seek a *drift*, which is a ford. It's another one of those words that pops up in place names.

A river basin or *catchment* refers to the area drained by a waterway, while the higher area that separates basins is the *watershed*. The *seep line* is a point on a slope where an impervious layer forces water to the surface. Soils on ridges above the seep line tend to be poor and sandy, and the bush less dense, making for nice walking terrain. Not so pleasant underfoot is a *vlei*, a marshy area where water gathers when rains are good. Like wildlife, walkers gravitate to *sodic pans*, which are common in the Kruger National Park and Kgalagadi Transfrontier Park, where a layer of impervious soil holds water that leaches mineral salts from the ground.

CAMP CHAT

Words from isiZulu infiltrate camp life as we hold an *indaba* or gathering in a *boma*, traditionally a fence of wood and thorns, in the shade of a *lapa*, a thatched shelter. And Afrikaans is heard at mealtime when the ambient scents herald *lekker kos* – delicious food. On the fire, *boerewors* is charring on a *braai* alongside *pap* or *bobotie* cooking in a *potjie*. If any of these words are novel, they won't be after a stay at a trail camp. If you retreat to your night quarters and find it has no corners then you are in a *rondavel*, the vernacular building of southern Africa.

Em Gatland

Guides join guests to chat around the campfire in Klaserie Private Nature Reserve.

THE WALKING SAFARI EXPERIENCE

Sally Lucas

Walkers follow their guide on animal-made trails at Manyeleti Game Reserve in the Kruger area.

MEET YOUR TRAIL GUIDE

One of the most rewarding benefits of swapping wheels for feet is the opportunity to spend time with the most interesting guides. The quality of a trail guide has a big influence on the walking experience, and in South Africa standards are high. In order to lead on foot in a big game area, trail guides require mandatory training and certification in addition to standard field guide qualifications. To earn these, the guides must log hundreds of hours in the veld and hundreds of close encounters with potentially dangerous animals.

Trail guides working in national parks may be full-time park employees or contracted professionals. SANParks and Ezemvelo KZN Wildlife employees follow their own training programmes, while almost all other guides are certified by the Field Guides Association of Southern Africa, the leading professional association (see the box on professional guide training on pages 28–29). In SANParks parks, many contracted trail guides are also members of the SANParks Honorary Rangers volunteer corps.

Most guides are men, but about 10 per cent of trail guides are women – and the number is growing. Although guiding is normally done in English, in the private sphere there are qualified guides who can lead groups in Afrikaans, German, French and Dutch; a request should be made in advance to check whether this can be arranged.

It needs a special character to be a good trail guide. After all, it is harder work than vehicle-based field guiding. Guides carry a heavy rifle in the heat, and are not allowed to

Denis Costello

RETURNAfrica

A pair of trail guides is the norm, and rifles are essential kit in big game areas.

use a shoulder strap in bushveld. They have the extra responsibility of keeping visitors on foot safe, and need the interpersonal skills to deal with any awkward guests. As well as having all the core guiding skills and a thorough knowledge of nature and bushcraft, good guides act as teachers to communicate information clearly.

Above all, the best trail guides have a genuine love for nature and can empathise with the excitement of a first-time trail walker. That said, even the finest of guides can tire of repeating information to a silent audience, and walkers will gain more from the experience by showing interest and asking questions. Occasionally it's possible to encounter a guide who is a bit unenthusiastic and would rather be doing something else, but almost all enjoy their work, are highly engaged, and delight in sharing their knowledge.

PRE-WALK PAPERWORK

At some point before setting out on a trail, participants will be asked to sign an indemnity form. At national parks it's best to ask for this on arrival at your camp, so that you can complete the form at leisure and not in the early hours just before leaving on a dawn trail.

An indemnity form asks for the names and ages of participants and for details about any medical conditions or infirmities they may have, and informs them of the risks involved. It also includes a section where walkers can mention special interests such as botany, birds or insects. In signing the form, participants confirm that they indemnify the park against any harm they may experience. Minors must have the form signed by a parent or legal guardian.

Before the walk starts, the guide will collect the forms, and may ask to see a medical letter of fitness from anyone over a certain age. In practice, for day walks guides seem to make a judgement call on the information walkers supply about their own levels of fitness.

PROFESSIONAL GUIDE TRAINING

The vast majority of professional guides working in the private sector, or under contract to national parks, have qualifications from the Field Guides Association of Southern Africa (FGASA). FGASA is accredited to provide guide training by the government training and certification body for the tourism sector, the Culture, Arts, Tourism, Hospitality and Sport Sector Education and Training Authority (CATHSSETA). It also facilitates the registration of guides with CATHSSETA, which is mandatory for trail guides working in South Africa.

Temba Brown qualified as a senior tracker at Bateleur Safari Camp in Timbavati Private Nature Reserve.

The actual training of guides is conducted by numerous private training providers that are endorsed by FGASA, and there are over 1,000 active qualified FGASA trail guides in the country, with certifications informally recognised throughout Africa.

The first step for an aspiring professional trail guide is to become a field guide, which allows for vehicle-based guiding and foot guiding in non-dangerous game areas. Sometimes you hear guides refer to their FGASA certification as Level 1, 2 or 3. This is a previous nomenclature, and today the qualification levels are known as Apprentice Field Guide, Field Guide and Professional Field Guide. At a minimum, guides must reach the first of these levels before going on to learn the skills to guide on foot in a big game area. There are four levels of trails certification: Apprentice Trails Guide, Trails Guide, Professional Trails Guide and Professional Special Knowledge and Skills (Dangerous Game).

A field guide who wants to do trails work must first attain a Level 1 First Aid Certificate, pass the FGASA Advanced Rifle Handling assessment, and take a theory exam. The aspiring guide then needs to log at least 50 hours as an observer on trails led by a qualified guide. During this time, he or she must also record a minimum of 10 encounters with a specified variety of big game animals.

ON THE TRAIL

Each walk in a big game reserve starts with a safety briefing. This is a good time to ask questions or let the guide know of any special interests you have. At this point, the guide is scanning the group and taking stock of its collective ability, to determine the distance and pace of the walk.

In areas with big game, trails usually have a lead guide and a back-up guide or 'second rifle'. The second guide is there partly for safety, but also as a way to give junior guides learning hours in the field. Don't assume that the guide at the front is the senior one: sometimes the junior guide takes the lead to work under the watch of the more experienced one. Based on conditions in a particular area, the wildlife present, or the time of year, there may be just one guide, or they may not be armed.

The next step requires the trainee to link up with an FGASA-approved mentor for 10 hours of one-on-one assessments. Passing this stage means the candidate has the right stuff to be a trail guide, and is ranked as an Apprentice Trails Guide. Further experience and training come in the form of field expeditions as 'second rifle' and then as 'first rifle' under the supervision of a mentor, clocking up at least 50 hours per role. With these hours logged, the trainee can start guiding paying guests, but only under the supervision of a fully qualified guide. This training process concludes with the FGASA VPDA (View Potential Dangerous Animals) Practical Assessment (see pages 148–149). If successful, the apprentice can finally qualify as a Trails Guide.

It will take some years for a working trail guide to achieve the FGASA Professional Trails Guide certification, which requires a minimum of 600 hours in the field and at least 300 dangerous game encounters logged. It is this level of commitment that results in such high levels of safety and quality in guiding in South Africa.

Working guides are encouraged to continue lifelong learning, adding certification in specialist areas such as tracking, biomes, birding and cultural guiding. With some of these under their belt, and more years in the field, a guide can reach the ultimate FGASA level – Professional Special Knowledge and Skills Dangerous Game (SKS DG). A guide who has attained both the SKS DG level and the Senior Tracker level can use the title FGASA Scout – and there are just a handful of these in Africa.

For more information, see the FGASA website, www.fgasa.co.za. Contact details are: tel: +27 (0) 11 886 8245; email: enquiries@fgasa.org.za

FGASA graduate Calvin de la Rey guides in the in the Kruger National Park.

Guides have a good knowledge of their area and its interesting features, but are explorers at heart, so every walk is different. The group walks silently in single file, usually with both guides at the front. That's because almost all animal encounters happen there, and this makes it easy for the guides to communicate quietly and deal with any situation. If one of the guides walks at the back for a while it might be a sign that someone in the group is stopping without telling the guides.

Silence is necessary because the guides need to listen for what may lie ahead, and also to avoid alarming the wildlife. The ideal animal encounter is one where walkers can observe the animal without detection. The group should stay together; there's no need to walk on the heels of the person ahead, just in a compact bunch so that if there is a sighting, everyone has a chance to see it. The guides should never be out of view.

Klaserie Sands

On most trails, two guides walk at the front and guests follow in single file.

Trail walkers are encouraged to swap positions in the line, as those near the front see more. Every 10 or 15 minutes, the lead guest should step to the side, let the others pass and continue at the tail. Walkers who need to stop for any reason should communicate this to the guides with a low whistle or tongue click, not by shouting or clicking fingers.

The guides will stop for interesting things such as tracks, dung, burrows, insects, special plants, birds and, of course, bigger animals. In most cases, it's not the goal of trail walking to seek out wildlife such as elephant, rhino, lion and buffalo; but encounters will happen and when they do, the guides will take a decision on the course of action. Depending on the situation – the type of animal, the number of them, the density of the bush – the guide may decide it's safe to go nearer, and sometimes wildlife can be approached up to a surprisingly close distance. It's important to stay still and quiet at an animal encounter. Apart from the primates, who can easily spot a human, the eyes of most animals are conditioned to detect movement, not to identify the shape of a human standing still.

Nature being nature, walks don't always live up to expectations. There's no guarantee of seeing anything, and animal sightings can be especially difficult if it's windy or the bush is thick. It's rare to find big cats while walking, and antelopes and other small mammals tend to be quite skittish around people on foot. The key to enjoying walks is to soak up the small things and treat anything else as a pleasant surprise.

SPOTTING AND TRACKING

Even for the most experienced hiker, walking in a big game area is different. We need to be ever alert, reading the landscape and soundscape. You may wonder why the guides are seemingly always a step ahead, and the first to spot an animal. It is not only that they are at the front, they are also relying on their experience and intuition. They have a finely developed feel for which animals are likely to be in which habitat. They know the plants that attract feeders and are acquainted with favourite resting spots. Guides are also familiar with the movement patterns of animals – when and where they seek water in the morning or evening. They know in which type of tree a species of bird likes to roost or feed. Even a particular bird may offer clues: seeing a number of oxpeckers can mean that buffalo are close.

Above all, guides use their acquired skills to detect which animals are nearby – primarily by listening for telltale sounds and looking at fresh spoor. Originally an Afrikaans word, the term 'spoor' is used to describe any evidence of an animal's presence, and includes tracks, dung, scent markings, scratch marks, bent, broken or nibbled vegetation, and disturbed ground where an animal has dug for food or minerals. Experienced guides even detect nearby animals by scent. Sound is vital; the alarm call of a bird or monkey can indicate a predator,

SANParks trail guide Obert Cubai deciphers tracks on the Napi Wilderness Trail in the Kruger Park.

and the crack of a big branch is an elephant feeding. Guides can detect the low grunts that lions use to communicate with their young.

While listening and scanning the bush, the guides also have an eye on the tracks as they walk. This is in itself quite a skill, and one of the most interesting aspects of walking safaris. Walkers learn not just which track belongs to which animal, but how fresh they are, how to estimate the size of the animal from the tracks, and the number of animals. Fresh spoor is of interest for safety reasons and allows for animal encounters under controlled conditions. Sneaking up on big animals is not advisable – in fact, guides will sometimes use sound or wind direction to warn animals of human presence, so that the animals aren't suddenly alarmed.

It can be fun to try to follow the fresh spoor of a leopard, lion, or rhino. The guide will weigh the merits of doing so; if the bush is dense, or the animal has young in tow, then the best decision would be to take another direction.

Professional trackers are not normally used on park walks, and most of their work is in the hunting sector, but some private reserves will employee them. The San (Bushman) people are especially renowned for their tracking skills and are sometimes invited to demonstrate their skills on privately operated walks.

TRAIL SENSE

By design, the reserves included in this guide have no managed trails. Walkers follow natural tracks made by animals and these are mostly a pleasure to walk, but they can be uneven, sandy, rocky, or strewn with thorn branches and piles of dung. The most basic trail hazard is a trip or fall, especially when trying to spot wildlife while on the move, or juggling a trekking pole, camera and binoculars.

South African bush is spikey – so don't be tempted to reach out to grab something to prevent a fall. Footwear needs to have a reasonably thick sole to protect against spines. If thorny bushes can't be avoided, then carefully use your hand or a trekking pole to move them to the side. Don't follow too close to the person in front, to avoid a branch whip. Another technique to protect yourself is to use a backpack as a shield, by reversing into the thorn branch and then swivelling through to the other side.

The shirt-snagging buffalo thorn is known as the 'wag-'n-bietjie' or 'wait a moment' bush.

Denis Costello

It's very unlikely that you will get a bite from a snake or a sting from a scorpion. Just don't go sticking your hands into holes in the ground or in trees, and take care if you are collecting firewood or turning over rocks and logs. And take a good look before sitting down.

Insects such as mopane bees are more of a nuisance than a hazard, but not overly so. For the most part, walking conditions are surprisingly benign given the many billions of insects in our surrounds. Watch out for biting ants – don't leave food lying around, and make sure it's wrapped or kept in Ziplock bags. It's amazing how quickly ants can find and infest any food left open. Leeches are not a common concern, as the conditions are mostly too dry for them to thrive here.

STAYING SAFE WITH WILDLIFE

The first job of a trail guide is to protect both their guests and the wildlife from harm. Reserve owners, walk operators and guides know that safety is paramount to the continued availability and success of walking safaris, and the safety record in South Africa is excellent.

Safety considerations come into play long before anyone puts on their boots, with intensive guide training and adherence to strict policies. When planning a walk, guides check the weather conditions, and will only go out when these are favourable. They will also determine a route that avoids unnecessary risks such as steep slopes, deep river crossings and thick bush. They know that guests want an enjoyable experience more than a physical challenge, and won't take chances that could result in a guest suffering from exhaustion or heatstroke.

There are five rules for keeping safe on trails, but one overarching one – to listen to the guide. This means paying attention to the briefing, and especially following directions when close to animals. The five rules are:

Guides will always give safety instructions when the group approaches big game.

Russell MacLaughlin

- Walk in single file.
- Keep silent while walking.
- Stay behind the rifles.
- Never run.
- Obey all commands without question.

In most cases, big game encounters happen in controlled conditions. Guides will detect an animal ahead and then indicate the plan to the group. If it's a herd of buffalo, a bull elephant in musth, predators feeding, or animals with young, the likely action will be to change direction to give the animals a wide berth and let them be.

Getting down low can make animals feel less threatened.

MORE Family Collection

The main risk while walking is an unexpected close encounter. Just about every animal can cause harm if they feel threatened or trapped, especially if they have young ones. Even an adult elephant can be hard to spot if the bush is thick or it's in a donga or riverbed. If the weather is windy, it makes the guides' job harder, as they depend on sound for warning.

In the case of a sudden encounter, the guides will talk quietly or use hand signals to indicate what they want the group to do: stop and stand still, move back, or get behind cover. It's important to always keep the guides between you and the animals. If an animal moves while the group is observing it, it may be necessary for the group to shuffle around a little to keep behind the guides.

Depending on the animal, guides may ask walkers to squat down. The lower profile of the human body may seem less threatening to a buffalo. However, a smaller profile might make a person look like prey to a big cat. The guides will have experience of many encounters and they are good at reading the body language of animals, knowing when it's safe to stay and when to go. Elephants in particular are very expressive, and are intelligent enough to read human body language, so it helps to show you are relaxed about meeting them. If told to move away by a guide, turn and walk steadily as a group, and never run.

If an animal moves aggressively towards the group, the guides will deal with it – watch for their signal and listen to the instruction. A guide can tell a mock charge from a real one. They may make a noise that gives the animal a surprise and causes it to stop or change direction. One method is to slide the bolt on their rifle. This is not a prelude to shooting – the metallic sound is confusing to the animal. They may even pick up a rock and throw it towards the animal.

Thankfully, serious injuries on guided trail walks are exceedingly rare in South Africa, but they do occur. Since escorted walking was introduced more than 60 years ago, there have been no visitor fatalities, but a trail guide lost his life to an elephant in iMfolozi in 2004.

Safety is not just for us humans, of course, but for the wildlife too. Some people feel uncomfortable about walking with armed guides, concerned that taking part in the activity might lead to an animal being shot. The risk of this is very, very low when the rules are followed. Guides are trained to lead trails as if they were unarmed, and use their skills and experience in reading the environment to avoid trouble. They don't go bashing about in the bushveld and then rely on the rifle to deal with the consequences. The discharge of a rifle is a highly unusual event, and when it happens it's a very big deal. The firearm is the insurance of last resort, and ultimately it's a condition for park authorities to allow public walking in big game areas. The human danger to wildlife comes as a result of climate change, habitat loss, poaching and speeding vehicles, and not from walking safaris.

A wildlife encounter at an unfenced camp is just as likely as one on the trail. The risks can be higher, as guides may be resting or guests may be inattentive to their surrounds, and after dark it's especially important to listen to the guide's instructions. There's no need to be unduly worried – every guide and many a guest has entertaining stories to tell of camp visitors, and it's part of the thrill of being in the wilds.

Charged by rhinos

Markus Jungnickel

In a moment the two white rhinos charged at us.

Up ahead, we spotted a white rhino cow and calf browsing on the levee of the White Umfolozi River. No other animal can look so fierce and yet be so gentle and lovable. The guide led us to within 30 metres, and we clustered behind a thorn bush and took some photos. Then, one of the visitors decided he'd like a different angle and moved towards another bush. Mistake number one. As soon as he stepped into the view of the rhinos, they became alarmed. Two seconds later, both charged at us.

Our lead guide immediately shouted and slid the bolt of his rifle. This noise was enough to make the animals swerve. But at the same time, several of our group panicked and ran. Mistake number two. Because now they were running directly into the new path of the rhinos. More shouting, and the guests braked and reversed, as the rhinos thundered past in a cloud of dust.

Later we talked about the lessons learned from this incident – how vital it is to follow the guide's instructions, to keep calm when something happens, and not to try to find the perfect place for a photo. I have found it best to stand a couple of metres behind a guide, looking over their shoulder. And if they turn, shuffle around so you are always at their back and not between the guide and the animal. **HM**

Unfortunately, poaching is a serious issue in South African reserves, and walkers may encounter evidence of poachers, including human tracks, snares and carcasses. In the unlikely event of spotting them, guides will never engage with poachers. Their top priority is to keep walkers safe, and to retreat and report.

Trail guides carry VHF radios or satellite phones for use in an emergency. Cell phones are not reliable for safety purposes, as network coverage is poor or non-existent in many wilderness areas. If the worst comes to pass, it's reassuring to know that South Africa has the best rescue services and medical facilities in Africa.

TAKING A REST

Before a walk starts, the guides usually have a good idea of where the group will take a break. They have a mental map of the best spots – a shady tree, a rocky outcrop, a waterhole view. It's a chance to cool down, rehydrate, have a snack and ask some questions. On a walking safari you will soon discover that the stops are the main thing, not the walking: it's surprising how much can be spotted while sitting. Sometimes a group can plod in the bush for an hour and see nothing, then sit for a while and magically animals start to appear.

Rest breaks provide a chance to slow down and enjoy the view.

It's tempting to leave biodegradable waste in the bush as, after all, an apple core or banana skin would be a delicious snack for bird or beast. But it's a bad idea. Firstly, it can build an association between humans and food. Severe problems have already been caused where wildlife has discovered this link, notably among baboons and vervet monkeys. Secondly, leaving food waste behind can inadvertently spread seeds. Finally, it violates the 'leave no trace' principle – nobody wants to see eggshells or orange peel left by previous walkers. Smokers should wait until there is a rest stop before lighting up, and carry a container to take away the filter with them.

It goes without saying that leaving any litter is a complete no-no. That includes toilet tissue, as in a dry habitat it will not break down and rot for many years. It's best to try to plan so there's no need to go to the toilet when on the trail, but sometimes this is unavoidable. If you need to do so, tell the guide before you go, and never sneak off without their knowledge. They will explain where to go – it will always be back in the direction from which the group has walked, never ahead. Keeping an eye out for any hazards such as snakes or scorpions, find a sandy spot and scoop out a hole with your boot. When you've finished, set fire to the toilet tissue with a lighter, and make sure every scrap is burned. If not, it will quickly be excavated by wildlife and scattered. Then bury the ashes by pushing sand over them and check that there are no exposed embers – accidental bush fires are a serious hazard in all habitats.

As well as not leaving anything behind, it is equally important that objects remain where you found them. As SANParks rules make clear: 'No plant, animal, wildlife or any natural or cultural items may be removed from the park without permission.' Whether it be a tortoise shell, a pot shard or merely a lovely feather, don't be tempted.

BEFORE YOU GO

MORE Family Collection

Walkers in Marakele National Park take time to admire a magnificent and ancient marula tree.

WHO CAN GO ON A TRAIL

Any active person can take part in walking safaris, but it's important to be aware of what to expect and pick a suitable one. Walks in this guide vary from short strolls of an hour to full-day hikes in tough conditions. A typical dawn walk will cover four to eight kilometres over three hours, with plenty of stops to examine interesting things or have a drink of water. Guides are careful to adjust the pace and distance to match the group's ability.

Wilderness trails are longer in duration and distance, and are more enjoyable if you are an active walker and reasonably fit. Backpacking trails are a further step up. Hikers need to be capable of covering up to 15 kilometres on a hot day with a full pack weighing 15 kilograms or more. For those not used to heat and humidity, it can be extra energy-sapping.

It's best to give the trail operator advance notice of any disabilities or health conditions that might impact on the feasibility of a walk. Because of the terrain, none of the walks in this guide are accessible to wheelchair users, or those with very limited mobility. Other disabilities do not preclude enjoyment of bush walks, especially in the private reserves and concessions where operators and guides can tailor the experience to match individual needs. In an area where close encounters with big game are likely, hearing impairment can increase the element of risk and should be discussed with the guide. For those with no or limited usable vision, bespoke walks are feasible everywhere, with the best options in the Western, Eastern and Northern Cape reserves where the risk is lower because of the open terrain and lower wildlife densities. In all cases, it's wise to discuss any concerns with the trail operator before making a booking.

Age limits

Taking children trail walking is a great way to create family memories. For SANParks the magic number is 12: that's the minimum age for all walks, and also the age from which adult accommodation rates apply. Under SANParks rules, walkers over 65 years of age are asked to bring a letter of fitness from their doctor. A standard form for trail participants over 65 is available from SANParks on request, designed to be completed and signed by a doctor.

In KwaZulu-Natal, Ezemvelo KZN Wildlife's rule is 'over 12' for day walks. They do not state a maximum age, but they request that walkers have a reasonable level of fitness and they reserve the right to reject participants if the trails officer feels that a person is not physically able to complete the trail. For Ezemvelo multi-day walks the minimum age is 14 if accompanied by a parent or legal guardian, and 16 if unaccompanied. Private trail operators can make their own rules, with the minimum age ranging from 12 to 16.

A San guide shares his knowledge with an eager learner in the Kgalagadi Transfrontier Park.

WHEN TO GO

As a big country with a diversity of climatic zones, there's somewhere to walk all year round in South Africa. That said, the summer is hot, and is also the time when there's statistically more rainfall in most regions. After good rains the bush can quickly thicken, and visibility becomes difficult. With more water sources thanks to the rains, animals tend to disperse and are no longer concentrated near rivers and waterholes. The autumn months – April to June – are generally the best months for walking. There's still enough green vegetation to make photos look good, and the chill of winter nights is yet to come. In Western, Eastern and Northern Cape parks, spring – September to October – is also an excellent walking season, with profusions of plants in bloom.

The high season for domestic tourism is over the summer months of November to March, reaching a peak around Christmas and New Year. SANParks does not have low/high-season pricing in general, but sometimes offers discounts for walking activities in the less popular hot months. Ezemvelo KZN Wildlife has different standard and high-season pricing for resorts, but this does not apply to trails.

Wilderness Leadership School

By May the rivers in Hluhluwe-iMfolozi Park are fordable, making it a good time to visit.

APRIL, MAY, JUNE

In the lowveld, April marks the start of the walking season with temperatures coming down from their summer peaks, which average in the high 20s and low 30s Celsius. If summer rains have been good, the bush is likely to be thick, restricting the range of areas that can be walked safely. April is one of the best times for birdwatching, with many migratory species in residence. The autumn months are very pleasant times for walking in the reserves of the Western Cape and Eastern Cape.

It's best to make bookings from mid-April to mid-June if possible, as school holidays run from mid-June to early July. The Easter weekend always falls just after a full moon, making it a great time for a wilderness escapade.

JULY, AUGUST, SEPTEMBER

Winter brings excellent walking conditions to most of South Africa. Day-time temperatures are favourable, with average highs in the low 20s Celsius in most of the country, and the bushveld starts to thin, making it safer for walking and easier to spot wildlife. It's a fine time to visit the reserves that are excessively hot for summer walking, such as the Kruger National Park and other lowveld reserves, Mapungubwe National Park and the Kgalagadi Transfrontier Park. Nights are near freezing point in the parks of the Northern, Western and Eastern Cape, so be prepared.

In mid-September, SANParks runs a 'Parks Week' during which it offers free day access to national parks for South African citizens and those with a residency permit, but this does not impact much on the availability of places on trails.

OCTOBER, NOVEMBER, DECEMBER

October is an excellent time for walking everywhere in South Africa. By November, rising temperatures start to make walking uncomfortable in all but the reserves of the Western and Eastern Cape. The spring months are the prime season for flora in the arid parks of the Karoo and Northern Cape. Most animals tend to give birth in early summer, so cute youngsters can be seen.

SANParks tariff increases for all national parks come into effect on 1 November annually, although some multi-day trails cost less at this time of year as their season winds down. After the first week in December, schools around the country close and it's peak holiday season until early January. By mid-December, most lowveld multi-day trails are closed.

JANUARY, FEBRUARY, MARCH

Statistically this period has the most rainfall, and if rains are good, the thicker bush makes it tricky to spot wildlife. For safety reasons, guides need to choose areas that are not too dense.

This is a great time to visit parks in the Western and Eastern Cape, where the summer heat is less intense, and multi-day trails are at their peak. In the rest of the country, these steamy months are the least attractive for extensive walking and many multi-day trails do not operate, while those that do may be discounted. That said, this is still a fine time to do a dawn walk before the daily heat and humidity set in. It's peak birding season in the lowveld, with many migratory species to be spotted. School holidays bring increased numbers of visitors to parks in late March.

Catherine Rodwell

October is a perfect time to set off in search of spring flowers in Gondwana Game Reserve.

Martin Klimko/Janine Salibova

Even in the summer heat, early morning walks in the Kruger Park can still be rewarding.

BOOKING BASICS

It's possible to take an impromptu decision to join a guided walk while in a park, but it's better to plan ahead, and essential for overnight trails. At popular camps, morning walks can fill up. At less visited camps and at private lodges, guides may need to be assigned to a group, or brought in for a specific booking.

In the following chapters, we give the names and websites of the operators of each walk experience and provide additional contact information for them at the end of the book (see pages 183–184). SANParks allows bookings up to 11 months in advance, and it's best to book multi-day trails early – especially the popular Kruger wilderness trails. Advance payment is always required. Payment by credit card is most convenient, or by bank transfer for domestic visitors. Cancellation fees vary, so check conditions and dates carefully when you make a booking.

The maximum number of guests on a walk in a big game area is eight, but some operators take no more than six. Even if a trail seems to be fully booked, it's worth checking in case there are cancellations. SANParks and Ezemvelo have minimum booking number requirements, and if a trail does not get the minimum number, walkers may need to switch to another trail or date. Private trails can generally cater for smaller groups.

Most wilderness trail camps are priced based on two people sharing accommodation, so are not optimal for solo hikers or odd-numbered groups. Private lodges usually offer a rate for single occupancy. The Kruger National Park's wilderness trails require each two-bed unit to be booked and paid for two, while Ezemvelo KZN Wildlife's wilderness trails are priced per person, so sharing with a stranger is a possibility for odd-numbered bookings. For backpacking trails where hikers provide their own tents, solo hikers are not at a disadvantage.

Some overnight trails only allow group bookings, but most are 'open'. Trail walking is great for groups of friends and it's of benefit when the group has a shared level of experience, ability and interests. On the other hand, it's also enjoyable to join an open trail and meet strangers from around the world with whom to share tales of wilderness walking experiences.

Zebra in Limpopo's Letaba Ranch Nature Reserve pause briefly to survey approaching hikers.

Klaserie Sands

Walks with SANParks and Ezemvelo KZN Wildlife normally require a minimum of four guests, but trails in private reserves, such as this one in Klaserie, do operate with fewer people.

SANParks Honorary Rangers

Backpacking trails require hikers to provide their own kit, making this type of trail the most affordable. Some also allow solo hikers to join booked groups.

MONEY MATTERS

All visitors to South African national parks must pay a daily conservation fee. For those who will spend more than a week in a year in any state-owned parks, it pays to subscribe to the annual SANParks Wild Card, which grants the holder free access to the parks but not discounts on accommodation or activities. The card is valid for walking safari destinations managed by SANParks, Ezemvelo KZN Wildlife, and Big Game Parks of the Kingdom of eSwatini. For South African residents, Ezemvelo also has its Rhino Card, valid only for its reserves in KwaZulu-Natal. There are three price levels of the Wild Card for residents of South Africa, residents of neighbouring Southern African Development Community (SADC) countries, and other international visitors. Couples (of any kind) can get a joint card, and there's also a family card. The Wild Card can be bought at park gates and is valid from the time of purchase. It can also be bought online, and the confirmation email, with the holder's ID, is enough to secure entry to the park. In private reserves, and some private concessions in national and provincial parks, a separate conservation fee applies, which is not covered by the Wild Card.

At private lodges, walking is usually part of the all-inclusive tariff – but not always, so ask about this when you make a booking. Private operators have more flexibility in their pricing than state organisations, and it is always worth checking their websites for special offers or requesting discounts for longer stays.

Walks in SANParks and Ezemvelo parks are priced separately from accommodation, with the rates published annually on their websites. When consulting this pricing information, note that the smaller bush camps and lodges in the Kruger National Park and Hluhluwe-iMfolozi Park may not list a tariff for walk activities, although these activities are generally available on request. SANParks also charge a 1 per cent community levy which applies to all overnight lodging and activities. Watch out for special offers on SANParks social media – large discounts are sometimes offered on Kruger National Park wilderness and backpack trails in the low season from late January through February.

A handful of the walks included in this guide can be done as a day visitor, but almost all require the participant to stay overnight in the camp or reserve. Each walk experience falls within a cost range which reflects the overnight cost on a 'per person per night' sharing basis (see the box opposite).

Walking safari costs are usually determined by the degree of luxury rather than the quality of the walk experience. SANParks's wilderness trail camps are neat, functional and affordable.

Klaserie Sands

High-end facilities, such as this trail camp in Klaserie Private Nature Reserve, pride themselves on stylish interiors and fine cuisine, and seeing to guests' every comfort.

In general, tipping is common in South Africa. In the hospitality sector, wages are low and tips are greatly appreciated. Private lodges often facilitate a pooled gratuity for camp staff, and separate tips for guides and trackers. Tipping at private lodges is the norm, and in state-owned parks tipping the trail guides is usual after multi-day walks, and at walkers' discretion for day walks. Trail guides have undergone additional training compared to other guides, often at their own expense, so being generous with tips will have a positive influence in encouraging more guides to get qualified and thus expand the number of reserves where walks are offered.

Buying travel insurance is a good idea, and some private trail operators will insist on guests having it. An accident on a trail may require helicopter assistance, and while rescue services in South Africa operate on a no-charge basis, cost recovery from insured overseas visitors is a reasonable expectation. Insurance will also ensure the best level of care if hospitalisation is needed.

COST CATEGORIES

Each walk experience listed in this book is costed on a per person per night rate. Four price categories are indicated, with most of the walk experiences falling into the lowest price category:

● under R1,500
● R1,500–R3,000
● R3,000–R6000
● over R6,000

There are no child rates for walks (children under the age of 12 are not allowed on these walks), and there are no known discounts for seniors.

MORE Family Collection

Guides and hikers discuss the finer details of life in the bush.

WHAT TO WEAR ON A WALK

For camouflage, bush walkers should wear neutral-coloured clothing – brown, green or khaki. Dark shades are better than light ones, as bright colours and white are not natural and will alert animals to your presence. A hat is essential, ideally one with a brim that protects your neck and ears from sunburn. A light buff is a handy item that can protect your face from dust during a drive; it can also be worn as a bandana or used to shield your neck from the sun.

Your footwear should be well tested before travel as a bad fit will ruin a trip. Hiking boots provide ankle support and are recommended for backpacking, but for other walks many people happily use trail shoes and find them cooler than boots. It's best to avoid sandals, and beware of low-quality footwear as summer heat can melt the glue on the soles. Short gaiters can be useful to stop grass seeds from infesting your socks; or wear low-cut socks instead of long ones, as the seeds are easier to remove from skin than from cloth or wool.

You'll need a medium-weight fleece for pre-dawn travel in open vehicles and for evening wear. In summer, bring a light waterproof coat or poncho to protect against showers. It's wise not to set off on a walk with too many layers, as after warming up they'll be a burden for the rest of the trail.

It's fine to wear shorts, leggings or breathable hiking pants. Jeans are adequate for short walks but not for longer trails, as they become too heavy in the heat or rain. If you're in doubt about what to wear, check this with the guides on the evening before the walk; they'll be able to tell you if there are ticks around, if the trails are thorny, or if rain showers are expected, and you can adjust your clothing to suit the conditions.

Look for unscented sunscreen and avoid using perfumes or strong-smelling soaps and creams, as the scents are easily detected by animals. It's best to leave any valuable jewellery at home.

Lowveld Trails Company

Walkers blend in with the environment while observing rhino in Timbavati Private Nature Reserve.

WHAT TO CARRY ON A WALK

It's essential to carry water on bush walks. When this is provided by the operator it's sometimes in the form of a disposable plastic bottle for each walker, so it's better to bring a reusable bottle and fill it at the camp. Outdoor equipment stores sell water containers and pouches with a shoulder strap which allows your hands to remain free, and the insulated versions will even keep a drink cool for a while. You shouldn't put ice in metal containers, because of the noise this will make while walking.

It's feasible to do without a day pack, and just carry a water bottle on a shoulder strap and binoculars or a camera on a harness. But it's better to have a small pack, preferably in neutral colours and with pockets for small items. The type of pack with an integrated hydration bladder is a handy option; alternatively it's good to have one with secure side pockets for easy access to water bottles. Useful items for the pack include sunblock, lip balm, personal sanitary items, hand sanitiser and a waterproof stuff sack in case of rain. Try to avoid Velcro fasteners and the noisy types of plastic bag; Ziplock bags are good for tissues and snacks. The pack should have space to stow a fleece after the day warms up, and to hold a light raincoat or poncho if this could be needed on the walk. It's sensible to take along a small personal first aid kit – a few blister plasters, antiseptic wipes and plasters, rehydration sachets and a pair of tweezers.

A day pack is useful for carrying snacks, water and personal items.

It's good to have some energy snacks in your pack, such as dried fruit, trail mix or muesli bars. Many walk operators supply snacks, either carried by the guide or distributed to walkers in advance. These typically include packets of fruit juice, biltong (dried meat), fresh or dried fruit, biscuits or energy bars.

Trekking poles should be considered, especially for multi-day wilderness and backpack trails. Apart from helping to distribute your body weight, they will help you keep your balance on river crossings and steep or loose surfaces.

Give some thought to what type of camera, if any, to carry on a trail. Modern cell phones can take excellent macro shots as well as landscape and group scenes, but don't forget to switch your phone to 'airplane mode' when out on foot – nothing would be more embarrassing than your phone sounding at a critical moment on the trail. Phones are not good for photographing birds and distant wildlife, but a big SLR camera can soon become burdensome on a walk, especially if it has a heavy zoom lens and assorted extra accessories. Realistically, the best wildlife shots will be taken from a steady perch on a vehicle, so you should consider leaving your camera behind and just taking binoculars. Alternatively, pack a small camera that can fit in a zippable belt pouch, one with an optical zoom of ×20 or ×30. Remember to turn off the camera sounds before leaving home.

It's harder to get close to wildlife on foot than in a vehicle, so binoculars are a must.

A pair of binoculars is an essential item for most walkers. A good size for walking is 10x42, although the smaller 10x25 will also do the job. It's best to keep them to hand, as an animal encounter is no time to be removing backpacks or fiddling with zippers. If your pack has a chest strap, you can tuck compact binoculars behind it while still having quick access to them. Lightweight harnesses are available that keep the equipment from swinging while you walk, and some harnesses have a neoprene pouch that protects equipment from dust and light rain.

On multi-day trails, it's recommended that you leave behind watches, phones, music players and other gadgets, and just enjoy a tech-free immersion in nature.

Most rest camps and lodges have mains power supplies for charging devices, and many trail camps have solar charging facilities. Plug sockets are either the European-style 2-pin (Type C) or the rounded three-pin unique to South Africa (Type M), and adapters are widely available.

HEALTH HAZARDS

Heatstroke and sunburn are the biggest walking safari health risks. Never set out without a hat, sun protection and plenty of water, and keep a few sachets of rehydration powder in your day pack. Secondary health hazards are insect bites and thorn scratches. They should be treated at the earliest rest stop with a wipe of an antiseptic swab.

The lowveld reserves, including the Kruger National Park and adjacent reserves, and those in the Kingdom of eSwatini, are year-round malaria risk areas, and Mapungubwe National Park and the KwaZulu-Natal parks have moderate summertime exposure to malaria. The mosquito risk is highest after dark, so keep tents zipped. Before travel to these areas, check with a doctor regarding anti-malarial precautions you should take.

Ticks can be an irritant, and tick bite fever is a risk in the lowveld. It's a bacterial infection (*Rickettsia africae*) characterised by an inflamed red sore at the bite location, and possible symptoms such as fever, headaches and a rash. Adult ticks are big enough to see, but the baby

Adult ticks are not hard to spot.

ones known as 'pepper ticks' are almost invisible. Ticks are found in grassland areas and are most common in the summer months, but with warmer winters are increasingly encountered year-round. You can help to protect yourself against tick bites by wearing high socks or long pants and using a DEET-based spray – a popular brand is Bayticol. Gaiters also offer some protection – preferably the ankle type, as knee-high gaiters can be too hot.

In camps, use a torch when moving around at night as snakes may be present. At unfenced camps, be sure to follow the guides' instructions regarding after-dark movements.

TRAIL TECH

- There are a couple of excellent (and pricey) mobile apps available for birding. Both *Roberts Multimedia Birds of South Africa* and *Sasol eBirds Southern Africa* are great for identification. The free, demo version of the Sasol app will give you a taste of the full version, but is restricted to just 30 birds. Both apps include bird calls, an additional aid to identification. Always check with your guide whether it is permissible to play bird calls while out on a walk. Using playback to lure birds can cause distress, particularly during the breeding season.

- There are wonderful free apps that turn your phone into a window on the night sky. Look for *Sky Map* for Android, or *Night Sky* for Apple iOS.

- A small solar charging panel is a useful addition to your kit when heading for off-grid trail camps. A folding model weighing about 750 grams can charge three USB devices at once.

- Because of the poaching risks, night vision equipment is not welcome in national parks. A UV torch is acceptable, and fun to use for finding scorpions, whose exoskeletons include a fluorescent substance.

- The use of drones in parks requires a detailed application process and payment of a hefty daily fee. Private reserves may allow drones to be used, subject to conditions such as that their use does not annoy other guests or wildlife.

SATourism/Janik Alheid

A mobile app will make reading the night sky easy and fun.

PACKING FOR BACKPACKING

It's worth giving some extra thought to your gear when heading into the veld with a full backpack. While it's not necessary to reach the level of sawing your toothbrush in half, careful planning, especially of meals, can shave a few kilograms off the load and make a multi-day trail much more enjoyable. A simple rule for what to include in your backpack kit is 'if in doubt, leave it out'. It's much more common to regret having carried something along than having left it behind. Pack the essentials, and only then consider including one or two luxuries. Use the table below as a checklist to help you.

ESSENTIALS	
Backpack	60–70 litres is a good size for a 3–4-day trip.
Tent	A single skin tent is suitable as long as it's opaque. Don't be tempted to use just an inner tent with a mesh, as lions can see through it.
Sleeping mat	This should be as lightweight and compact as possible.
Sleeping bag	A one- or two-season bag (5°C) is fine for most of the year, and a three-season bag (0°C) during winter.
LED head torch	This is an essential item, so bring spare batteries.
Camping stove, accessories and fuel	Gas canisters are lighter than liquid fuel. The smallest size (100 grams) can be hard to find – Camp & Gas in Mbombela (Nelspruit) is a reliable source if you're travelling to the Kruger National Park.
Utensils	These should include a bowl, mug, fork and spoon (or spork), and a camp knife or multi-tool.
Water containers	Set off with a minimum of two litres in bottles or bladders, and at least the same again in storage capacity for use at the camp.
Water purification	Chlorine drops and tablets can be bought at pharmacies or outdoor equipment stores. A filter is not usually required, but it's worth having just in case. The Sawyer Mini Filter is a good option.
Sun protection	A hat with a brim, sunblock and lip balm, as well as sunglasses if desired.
Anti-insect lotion	A DEET-based cream or spray. If you prefer a DEET-free lotion, look for alternatives such as Natrapel 8 Hour and Picaridin.
Wash kit	The soap in the wash kit should be biodegradable.
Camping towel	A lightweight microfibre towel. A smaller towel is also useful for cleaning and drying your feet after a river crossing.
Toilet tissue and lighter	Pack these in a Ziplock bag. Guides usually provide a small shovel or auger for bush toilets.
First aid items	Guides carry a first aid kit, but it's useful to have a small personal one to treat sprains, cuts, or blisters.
Personal medicines	Include malaria prophylaxis if required in the area where you will be walking.
Compressible stuff sacks	A waterproof sack to keep electronic items dry. A sack for dirty clothes and another one to carry out rubbish.

Hike clothing	This should include breathable hiking gear in dark earth colours, a swimsuit if river bathing will be an option, and a set of spare underwear and socks for each day.
Evening clothing	Long pants or leggings, a fleece top, and a beanie or other cap and gloves in winter.
Trail boots	While trail shoes can be fine for most walks, the added weight you carry when backpacking means that boots with ankle support are needed.
Camp shoes	Light sandals or lightweight shoes for evenings at camp.
Camp meals	Outdoor stores such as Cape Union Mart, Trappers and Outdoor Warehouse carry hiking meals. Ziplock bags of muesli pre-mixed with milk powder make a good breakfast.
Snacks	Biltong, energy bars, hard-boiled eggs, crackers, dried fruit and nuts.
Drinks	Tea bags or sachets of hot chocolate or coffee. Powdered juice such as Oros or Amila to flavour water.

NON-ESSENTIALS

Vacuum-packed meat	Some guides allow guests to cook on the fire – check with them first. A butcher will cube and vacuum-pack meat for you and it will last for a few days.
Treats	At the end of a hard day, it's nice to have a reward such as a hip flask with a favourite drink, chilli sauce, or sweets.
Rain gear	If rain is forecast, bring a poncho or light waterproof.
Compact binoculars	They should have a harness to stop them swinging.
Camera	To be useful the camera will need to have a good optical zoom. Add a spare battery or solar charger, and a gorilla tripod for night shots.
Gaiters	Ankle-high gaiters are helpful to keep grass seeds, dust and ticks off your socks and feet.
Trekking poles	These can be useful at river crossings and on loose slopes.
Repair kit	This can include a sewing kit, and duct tape for ad hoc repairs to boots, sleeping mattresses and other kit. Instead of carrying a whole roll of duct tape, a metre of it can be stored wrapped on a trekking pole.
Solar charger	Bring this if you'll need to charge a camera or phone.
Camp chair	The tripod type of chair is light enough to carry.
Pocket shower	A lightweight 10-litre bag with a shower head and cord for suspension from a tree.
Day pack	Sometimes a backpacking camp stays put for two nights, in which case it's useful to have a light day pack for snacks, water, a camera and swimwear.
Flour sack	It's hard to stay clean on a trail. A flour sack weighs little and can be stuffed into a side pocket of your pack, and used when sitting or lying on the ground. It's also useful for packing up rubbish at the end of a trail.

Denis Costello

Wilderness trails in the iMfolozi section of the Hluhluwe-iMfolozi Park are memorable for the splendid lookouts along the way.

Located in north-eastern KwaZulu-Natal in the heartland of the former Zulu Empire, about 280 kilometres north-east of Durban, Hluhluwe-iMfolozi Park is one of South Africa's most pristine wilderness areas. It includes the first areas conserved by law in South Africa, with Hluhluwe and iMfolozi having been proclaimed in 1895. Before then, the area was settled by the Mthethwa clan under the Zulu leader Dingiswayo, and in the early nineteenth century King Shaka used the lowlands between the White and Black Umfolozi rivers as his private hunting ground. The remnants of his hunting pits, used to trap large numbers of game at a time, can still be found near Siyembeni, the confluence of the two great rivers towards the east of the iMfolozi section of the park. In the west lies Nqolothi Hill, where the king sat to oversee elephant hunts.

In 1989 the Hluhluwe and iMfolozi reserves were joined to form one park containing almost 100,000 hectares of wilderness. In 2019, community-owned lands abutting the park south of the White Umfolozi River were designated for conservation as the uMfolozi Big 5 Reserve, further extending the protected area. iMfolozi, Umfolozi, uMfolozi and Mfolozi are all variants of the names of the rivers at the heart of the western section, and park authorities use the Umfolozi spelling for the rivers, and iMfolozi for the reserve itself. The name is derived from *mfulawosi*, an isiZulu word meaning 'rivers of fibre', which is believed to refer to mountain nettle, a fibrous plant that grows along the river banks and is used for making mats. *Hluhluwe* (pronounced 'klu-klu-wee') is the isiZulu name for Hluhluwe creeper, a thorny, rope-like climbing plant that can be seen alongside the short trail in Hilltop Camp.

The park's soils are derived from eroded volcanic, glacial and sedimentary rocks and allow for a considerable diversity of plants and grasses which, in turn, provide sustenance and shelter for a great variety of animals and birds. The most dominant trees are knob thorn, sweet thorn and umbrella thorn.

Today, the park is synonymous with the white rhino, as it was here that the last of these animals faced extinction by the late nineteenth century. From the early 1960s, under the leadership of Ian Player, the remnant population was saved in 'Operation Rhino', which saw the development of safe animal darting and transport techniques that led to the distribution of a sustainable population of rhino to other reserves. Only the Kruger National Park has more white rhino than Hluhluwe-iMfolozi, although all reserves are struggling to contain the upsurge in poaching. As well as black and white rhino, elephant, buffalo, nyala, greater kudu, red and blue duiker, bushbuck, impala, zebra, blue wildebeest, steenbok and giraffe are likely to be spotted. Predators present include cheetah, spotted hyena, leopard and lion. More than 350 bird species have been counted in the reserve, making it an excellent birding destination. Noteworthy species include the African finfoot, Narina trogon, southern ground-hornbill and white-backed night heron.

WALKING IN HLUHLUWE-IMFOLOZI PARK

Hluhluwe-iMfolozi has a humid, subtropical climate. Temperatures are good for walking year-round, but it's preferable to avoid the wetter summer months. The winter time offers perfect daytime conditions, but nights are chilly. The best months are April to July after the rains, while September is also a top month. November is when the higher humidity and heat arrive. Visitors need to bring protection against ticks, especially in summer.

The park has an excellent selection of walking options, second only to the Kruger National Park. It is not possible to do walks as a day visitor, but there is a range of options for overnight guests that includes day walks, wilderness trails and backpacking trails. It's a hilly park, so reasonable fitness is required. Day walks are available from lodgings throughout the park, but all multi-day trails operate in the western part, iMfolozi. There, the river valleys and watershed west of the confluence of the Black Umfolozi and White Umfolozi rivers form the core of a large wilderness area with no wheeled access. The rugged terrain makes for interesting trails with dramatic viewpoints.

The park is operated by Ezemvelo KZN Wildlife, which offers a variety of accommodation options at two resorts, Hilltop and Mpila, as well as a number of bush camps, lodges and safari tent camps in both sections of the park. Most walks in the park are operated by Ezemvelo. Rhino Ridge Safari Lodge is a private concession in the Hluhluwe section that offers day walks, while the Wilderness Leadership School does not have any fixed accommodation in the park but runs backpacking trails in the iMfolozi section.

The closest entrance to Hluhluwe-iMfolozi is at Nyalazi Gate, a three-hour drive from Durban. From there, guests should allow an hour to reach Hilltop Resort or Rhino Ridge in Hluhluwe, or Mpila Resort in iMfolozi.

Denis Costello

Trails officer Mphile Mthethwa (back) walks with author Hlengiwe Magagula on a wilderness trail.

EZEMVELO KZN WILDLIFE WALK EXPERIENCES

Ezemvelo KZN Wildlife operates day walks from resorts and bush camps in both sections of the park, and a number of wilderness and backpacking trails in the iMfolozi zone. The southern half of iMfolozi is a designated wilderness that can only be accessed on foot; this area is the spiritual home of wilderness trails in South Africa, offering walkers the opportunity to immerse themselves in overnight trails in a pristine environment.

The gateway to all Ezemvelo multi-day trails is the Mndindini Trails Camp on the White Umfolozi River. From here, walkers explore the river valley in both directions, sometimes hugging the banks amidst tall stands of reeds. The rivers are broad and meandering and generally easy to cross, unless there has been heavy rain in the catchment.

A particular feature of hiking here is the opportunity to climb to krantzes high above the river, to enjoy viewing the wildlife behaving naturally and undisturbed. Mahobosheni (the isiZulu name for the puff adder) is a vantage point where the Umfolozi doubles back, forming a shape like a snake's head. A little further upriver is Nqabaneni, meaning 'fortress', and nearby is a cave with interesting erosion patterns, a good place for a shady rest with a view. Another splendid lookout is known as Shaka's Rock, said to have been used for the execution of enemies during the rule of King Shaka.

Over the decades, Ezemvelo has developed a selection of wilderness trail formats with a variety of durations and difficulty levels. They can be divided into three types based on the features of the overnight facility: a bed in a permanent camp, a mattress in a tent, or a sleeping bag under the stars.

Denis Costello

Guests make for the shade of a sycamore fig on a walk led by Ezemvelo KZN Wildlife trails officers.

There are no chairs or tables at the camps, but cushions are supplied, making for comfortable seating after the day's walking is done.

The most comfortable trail type has walkers based at the Mndindini Trails Camp, and this is known as the Base Camp Trail. Mndindini is a fixed camp that has tents with beds, dining tables and benches, showers and flush toilets. In terms of camp comfort, it is at a similar level to a SANParks Kruger National Park wilderness trail (see the box on SANParks Wilderness Trails on pages 84–85).

The second type of trail is the standard Wilderness Trail, where walkers are based at tented fly camps, with supplies transported to the camp by donkey. Each walk season, a new fly camp is established, always close to the river. Participants stay in the camp for the duration of the trail, which is run over two or three nights. The camp has two-person dome tents furnished with mattresses and pillows. There are no chairs or tables, but camp cushions are provided, which are quite comfortable when propped against a log. Water is sourced from the river and transported to the camp by donkey. It is filtered for drinking and cooking, and heated over a campfire so that hikers can take a warm shower. For toilet needs, a short shovel is provided, and instructions are given about where to go.

The third type, called the Primitive Trail, is the most demanding trail and has groups backpacking and sleeping under the stars. Hikers take turns to keep watch by a small fire at night, making it one of the most authentic walking safari experiences to be had in South Africa. A high level of fitness is required to deal with heavy packs, heat, long distances and the night watch.

Finally, it's possible to combine the Base Camp and Primitive Trail experiences in the Explorer Trail. This is a good option for those who have a long drive to reach the park, as the first and last nights are spent at the Mndindini Trails Camp.

Day walks and wilderness trails are led by a trails officer, while wilderness trails include an additional guide to assist. On Ezemvelo walks the 'second gun' usually follows at the back, unlike the practice in the rest of South Africa, where both guides walk at the front of the group. This is because the thick bush in the park can make it hard for the lead guide to keep all the guests in sight, and the second guide helps to make sure the group stays close together.

Day walks

Ezemvelo KZN Wildlife runs day walks from all resorts and bush camps in Hluhluwe-iMfolozi Park. In summer, dawn walks depart at 05:30 and in winter at 06:00. They last between 2.5 and 3 hours. Afternoon walks depart at 15:30 and last around 2.5 hours. Walkers meet the guide at a designated point, and it's usual to drive some distance in a game-viewing vehicle, varying the start locations.

■ Walk type	Day walk
■ Booking	www.kznwildlife.com
■ Cost category	Under R1,500
■ Group size	3–8
■ Min. age	13
■ Season	January–December

From Hilltop Resort, typical walks explore the bushveld in the environs of the resort, and the slopes down to the Hluhluwe River. When the veld is dense and thorny, the walk progresses at a sedate pace, with plenty of time to admire the views as the guide describes the variety of grasses, flowers, shrubs and birds.

The park does not take advance bookings for day walks. Guests should make accommodation bookings, then enquire about walks at the reception of Hilltop or Mpila Resort. If there are enough participants and a guide is available, the walks can take place – dawn walks are more popular than afternoon walks. Nselweni Bush Lodge guests should book and pay for walks at Mpila Resort. The smaller Ezemvelo KZN Wildlife bush lodges are bookable on a private group basis and include the services of a cook and a field guide for walks, which are offered at no additional fee.

Watched by a white rhino and her calf, lead trails officer Sinothi Ntombela explains all.

EZEMVELO KZN WILDLIFE MULTI-DAY TRAILS: TOP TIPS

- The trails schedule is available online at www.kznwildlife.com, and it shows departure dates and current availability. The park will email the schedule on request – contact mftrails@kznwildlife.com.

Tamboti and ironwood are campfire favourites, and the dead wood is gathered at a distance from the camp to reduce the environmental impact.

- Price changes occur in November, so if you're checking early in the year, the availability dates for November and December may not show, as the pricing for those months may not yet have been finalised.
- All multi-day trails require check-in at Mpila Resort. For pricing details of the trails and accommodation at Mpila Resort, look for the Tariffs section on the website.
- The cheapest trail option is the two-day Short Wilderness Trail, and the most costly is the Base Camp Trail.
- The trails need a minimum of four participants, except for the Primitive Trail and Explorer Trail, which have a minimum requirement of six people. Hikers who book one of the trails and find that the minimum numbers are not reached can request a refund, switch trails, or ask the park to try to accommodate them at Mpila or Hilltop where they can go for day walks.
- To preserve the wilderness experience, guests are requested not to bring electronic gadgets and watches with them. These can safely be left in cars at the Mndindini Trails Camp.

Wilderness Trails

There are two wilderness trail options, the only difference being their duration – two nights for the Short Wilderness Trail and three nights for the Extended Short Wilderness Trail. The same fly camp is used for both trail options, with the Short Trail starting on Fridays and Sundays and the Extended Short Trail starting on Tuesdays. Both trails run from mid-February to early December.

Walk type	Wilderness trail
Booking	www.kznwildlife.com
Cost category	Under R1,500
Group size	4–8
Min. age	16, or 14 if accompanied
Season	February–December

For wilderness trails, it is recommended that participants stay at Mpila Resort the night before the trail begins so that overnight gear can be handed over to be ported by donkey. The donkeys leave early on the starting day, and if hikers don't overnight at Mpila they need to carry their kit on the first day of walking. Either way, it's wise to keep your pack light and take only the essentials needed at the camp – wash kit, camp towel, a change of clothes. Take a day pack for water, snacks and any personal items you may need while walking.

On the first day of a trail, hikers meet the guides at reception in Mpila Resort by 11:00 for departure at 12:00. After a chat, they follow the ranger's vehicle for seven kilometres to Mndindini Trails Camp in their own vehicles. The road, which is closed to other park visitors, is accessible to sedan cars. At the base camp there is secure parking and toilet facilities, and belongings not needed on the trail can be left in the car.

A pause in the shade allows for bush lessons from trails officer Sinothi Ntombela.

Denis Costello

After a day in the wilds, a bucket shower of warm river water is very welcome.

Markus Jungnickel

After a snack and a briefing, the walk starts. The fly camp supply donkeys will already have left from Mpila Resort, so hikers don't walk with them. The distance walked on the first day varies, as the camp is at a different site each season, and because the guides may take a circuitous route to get there.

Trails are fully catered, with all meals prepared by a camp cook. Breakfast dishes typically include cereal, bacon and eggs. After breakfast, walkers collect their lunch packs which may contain sandwiches of cheese, salami and tomato, as well as fruit, crackers and biltong. A typical evening meal might be pap (mealie meal porridge) and stew or spaghetti bolognese with corn on the cob and a side salad, followed by tinned peaches and custard for dessert. Water filtered at the camp is made available in a canister for refilling personal water bottles.

On the second day walking begins early, and each guest takes a lunch bag and water in their day pack. The guides will decide on the trail route depending on conditions and hikers' interests. There are some fine lookout points above the river, providing excellent opportunities for a long and leisurely lunch break and wildlife spotting.

The group returns to camp in the early afternoon, picking up wood on the way back for the campfire. Water is heated in a cauldron over the fire, and hikers shower from a bucket rigged from a tree a discreet distance from the camp.

Early on the final day, the donkeys return to take away the guests' bags and waste. Meanwhile the group walks back to Mndindini Trails Camp, to arrive by 10:30 at the latest.

Base Camp Trail

For those who like a little extra camp comfort, the three-night Base Camp Trail is the one to pick. Located at the White Umfolozi River, the unfenced Mndindini Trails Camp has fixed tents on wooden decks, and communal ablution facilities with hot and cold showers and flush toilets. Each tent has two beds and bedding, and the camp has a shared fridge for cold drinks.

■ Walk type	Wilderness trail
■ Booking	www.kznwildlife.com
■ Cost category	R1,500–R3,000
■ Group size	4–8
■ Min. age	16, or 14 if accompanied
■ Season	February–December

As with the wilderness trails, there is a cook at the camp, so the trail is fully catered, with dining at bench tables in the kitchen area. Hikers' vehicles remain nearby, so there's no need to stress about something vital left behind.

Walkers, carrying just a day pack, set off after an early breakfast and return to the camp by lunchtime. The trails officer decides on the route, which can range from seven to fourteen kilometres depending on conditions and group preferences. The walks explore a different area to any contemporaneous wilderness trails, so that groups won't see each other in the bushveld.

Keen hikers can request another walk in the afternoon. Otherwise the camp is a pleasant place to relax and watch waterbuck, elephant and buffalo at the river. On the final day, there is a shorter morning walk, and the trail ends before 11:00.

The Base Camp Trail runs two or three times a month, each trail spanning a weekend, from mid-February to early December.

For most of the year, crossing the White Umfolozi River is easy.

Markus Jungnickel

The view from Nqabaneni

From our rocky outcrop, high above the river, the landscape was vast, still and apparently empty. Then, a movement – an antelope lifting its head – and my eye adjusted to the scale. Five, six ... fifteen bushbuck, their hides the same muddy grey-brown as the river bank. A shadow under a tree shifted, and revealed itself – a white rhino, avoiding the midday heat.

We were on the second of four days on the iMfolozi Wilderness Trail in Hluhluwe-iMfolozi Park and had discovered that just sitting and waiting is a rewarding way to enjoy the natural world.

These trails are an opportunity to step outside the confines of a vehicle and gain a richer experience. We picked the three-night Extended Short Wilderness Trail. The trail is designed to be as accessible as possible; our overnight gear had been transported by donkey to a camp, so we just had the essentials to carry – water, sun protection, camera and binoculars. The camp is fixed in one location for the season and each day we ventured out into a different area.

It was soon clear how vital the river is, even in the dry season when it's ankle deep. On the first and last days, our walk stayed close to the bank, with several crossings. Concentration was required, as it's here that big animals like to browse. As well as having a sixth sense for what lay ahead, Sinothi Ntombela – our trails officer – had the experience to know how close we could approach. A dozen buffalo were given a wide berth; so too, a bull elephant in musth, a hormonal state that makes them cranky.

Denis Costello

Nqabaneni, meaning 'fortress', is one of the many vantage points
overlooking the White Umfolozi River.

The second day followed a similar pattern. After breakfast in camp, we meandered for a couple of hours through the bush. The route we walked that day rose gradually. Away from the river, the sound of birds was replaced by the crunch of dry leaves under our feet and we walked silently for an hour without seeing any animal movement.

Bonding is easy after three days of sharing a trail.

With the White Umfolozi River carving through a deep valley, the topography suits the 'sit and watch' style of wildlife spotting. By midday we had reached the perfect location: a small tamboti tree for shade, and a panoramic view. A couple of hours passed easily, as nature revealed itself below. In the river, a lone elephant scooped muddy water onto its back. Beyond, a male rhino, then another. Although not immune to the current poaching crisis, Hluhluwe-iMfolozi has one of the most concentrated populations of rhinos in Africa.

Our guides, Sinothi and his 'second rifle', Mphile Ntombela, were veterans of many walks, and their enthusiasm was undiminished. Thanks to their reassuring presence, we gradually stopped worrying about an unexpected encounter with a big animal, and began to appreciate experiences impossible to have from the seat of a car: the feel of a bleached skull showing the perfect fit of a hippo's incisors; following the fresh track of a leopard at sunrise. The trees, at first a blur of thorn and leaf, became distinct, each with its own story and evocative name: tamboti and leadwood, fever-berry and knobbly creeper, the shepherd's tree, perfect for a shady rest.

A pause near the river was a chance for Mphile to remind us of the upcoming Umhlanga festival, when the reeds are harvested by maidens for traditional ceremonies. I nodded along, as it's also the biggest cultural event of the year in my Swati homeland.

By late afternoon, we had each got our own bucket of brown river water, warmed in a potjie, for a welcome bush shower. The camp is designed to have a low environmental impact. On the return walk we gathered firewood at some distance. The toilet facility was minimal and bush-friendly – a shovel and a lighter. At the end of each season, the campsite is returned to the wilderness without human trace, and a new location is selected in the following year. **HM**

Primitive Trail

The Primitive Trail comes close to how humans have experienced the bush in big game country for aeons – sleeping under the stars and taking turns at the night watch by a low fire. This trail has three- and four-night options. Similar to the Kruger National Park's backpacking trails, hikers have to carry everything they need, choose their campsite for the night and leave no trace (see box on SANParks backpacking trails on pages 96–97). Unlike the Kruger trails though, tents are not used, and the trail is fully catered, with guides and guests sharing cooking duties. If necessary, backpacks, sleeping bags and sleeping mats will be supplied, at no additional cost. When booking, participants will be asked to indicate what they need, but it's better to bring your own gear if you have it. If rain is forecast, a tarpaulin is carried to be rigged between trees. Water is collected from springs or rivers, and guests are advised to bring purification drops. It's a good idea to bring a swimsuit for river bathing.

It's wise not to underestimate the

Walk type	Backpacking trail
Booking	www.kznwildlife.com
Cost category	Under R1,500
Group size	6–8
Min. age	16, or 14 if accompanied
Season	February–December

When sleeping outdoors, it's vital to pick a spot that is safe from wildlife traffic.

Denis Costello

difficulty of this experience. Distances on the Primitive Trail can be up to 20 kilometres in a day, and on a four-night trail hikers must be prepared to carry over 20 kilograms. The guides have 8–10 favoured camping locations close to water sources, and they will select a location depending on the ability of the group and the weather conditions. The group may move to a new camp each night, or stay in the same spot for a couple of nights. Care is taken to hike in a different area to any other groups on the various trails at the time.

Cooking is done over a campfire by the guides, and participants are expected to help with preparing the food, washing dishes and pots, and digging for water when necessary. The food selection is not as rich as on the other trails, but always adequate and tasty. Fresh meat is buried in wet sand to keep it cool.

This trail has a minimum booking requirement of six people in order to facilitate the night watch safely. It runs every week from mid-February to early December. Participants should check in at Mpila Resort by 09:30, which is earlier than the other trails. Before the start of the trail, the food and utensils are shared out for each member of the group to carry. As with the other trails, participants drive themselves the seven kilometres from Mpila to Mndindini Trails Camp following the guide vehicle. On the final day the group will be back at their cars at Mndindini by 10:00 at the latest.

Explorer Trail

The Explorer Trail is a combination of the Base Camp Trail and Primitive Trail experiences. It lasts four nights, and hikers spend the first and last nights at the base Mndindini Trails Camp, with all its relative comforts. It's a nice option for those who have a long journey to reach the park, providing a restful first night, and the chance of a hot shower after the trail ends. Participants should check in at Mpila Resort by 13:00, with the aim of reaching Mndindini by 14:00. Guests drive their own vehicles to Mndindini, so the first night there provides an opportunity to repack for the backpacking nights and leave everything else in the car.

■ Walk type	Backpacking trail
■ Booking	www.kznwildlife.com
■ Cost category	Under R1,500
■ Group size	6–8
■ Min. age	16, or 14 if accompanied
■ Season	February–November

The second and third nights are spent sleeping in the wild, just as on the Primitive Trail. These nights may be at two different locations or at the same location. As no tents are used, hikers take turns to keep solo night watch by the campfire, regularly patrolling the surrounds with a torch to watch for wildlife. It's both a responsibility and a genuine wilderness experience. At the Mndindini base camp, meals are prepared by the camp cook, while on the other nights the trail guides cook with the help of guests.

The Explorer Trail operates two or three times per month from late February to late November on dates published by Ezemvelo (see the box on Ezemvelo KZN Wildlife Multi-day Trails on page 55). Like the Primitive Trail, it needs a minimum of six participants in order to manage the night watch rota.

Denis Costello

Early morning is a good time to swap yarns with trails officer Jabulani Thethwayo.

WILDERNESS LEADERSHIP SCHOOL

Hluhluwe-iMfolozi holds a special place in the history of public escorted walking in African reserves, as it was here that park ranger Dr Ian Player and his friend and colleague Magqubu Ntombela led South Africa's first wilderness trail on 19 March 1959. Dr Player succeeded in having an area of 12,000 hectares designated as a wilderness zone within the park – a first on the African continent – and today it continues to boast the most authentic wild trail experiences available in any South African national park.

While working in the park in the early 1960s, Player established the non-profit Wilderness Leadership School (WLS) with the goal of incubating a love for the wilderness in future leaders. In the beginning, the WLS brought groups of school children on trails in St Lucia Reserve and what was then the Umfolozi Reserve. Headquartered in Durban, the WLS today continues to operate trails in exactly the same way as Player did, and has extended its operations to reserves in other parts of South Africa and Botswana.

In iMfolozi, the WLS operates trails exclusively in the Black Umfolozi River valley, while Ezemvelo KZN Wildlife trails stick to the White Umfolozi area. About 40–50 per cent of WLS trails are for school groups, with most of the rest of the trails run for specialist groups, leadership training and personal development groups. The general public is welcome too, as the WLS has regular 'open trails' throughout the season that anyone can join. The school also runs guide training for FGASA accreditation (see the box on professional guide training on pages 28–29).

■ Walk type	Backpacking trail
■ Booking	www.wildernesstrails.org.za
■ Cost category	Under R1,500
■ Group size	6–8
■ Min. age	15
■ Season	January–December

The Wilderness Leadership School runs trails that introduce young people to the wonders of the wilderness.

The WLS operates trails year-round, but more frequently in the peak season of May to October. The school supplies all necessary hiking kit, and participants need to be prepared to carry a heavy pack. Food is included, and meals are of a high standard.

With no fixed camps, the format is the same as the Ezemvelo Primitive Trail, but more flexible in duration. The most popular WLS trail option is a four-night, five-day stay, and a package is available that includes transport from Durban.

Ian Player believed in the spiritual benefit of the solitary night watch, and insisted upon it being part of the routine for all wilderness trail walkers. This ritual continues today on WLS trails, and the experience of sitting alone by a small fire, immersed in the nocturnal sounds of the wild, creates an unforgettable memory.

RHINO RIDGE SAFARI LODGE

Rhino Ridge Safari Lodge is a comfortable, privately operated lodge built on community-owned lands that have been incorporated into the park. It offers walks throughout the year at an additional fee. The lodge location is terrific, perched on a hill on the northern boundary of the Hluhluwe section. There are two ways to reach it; the recommended route traverses the park for 31 kilometres from Nyalazi Gate and takes an hour, as it is partly on gravel road.

Dawn walks are led by one or two armed guides, and last about three hours. Afternoon walks are also possible and depart at 15:00 after high tea. Those aged over 65 should bring a doctor's certificate of fitness. Although the area around the lodge is hilly, the walks are not too demanding and aim to keep in areas of thin bushveld and grassland. There's a good chance to come close to rhinos on foot.

Walks outside the park boundary are also offered. One two- to three-hour walk explores the nearby Ndimbili Gorge; as there's no dangerous game on this walk, children from 10 years are allowed. There is also a cultural walk which takes in nearby Zulu homesteads, offering the opportunity to learn about traditional life, crafts and bush medicine, and homestays can be arranged.

Isibindi Africa Lodges

April to October brings the best walking conditions to Hluhluwe-iMfolozi Park.

▦ Walk type	Day walk
▦ Booking	www.rhinoridge.co.za
▦ Cost category	R3,000–R6,000
▦ Group size	2–8
▦ Min. age	16, or 14 if accompanied
▦ Season	January–December

Barefoot biophilia in Zululand

Isibindi Africa Lodges

Trail guide Nunu Jobe is known as the rhino whisperer.

Nunu Jobe is biophilic. Don't worry, he is quite okay and does not need a cure. Biophilia is a lovely word. It describes something innate in humans, the 'love of life or living systems'. It recognises that the human species is but one among millions of life forms, and that our collective well-being is interwoven. Nunu is the embodiment of biophilia. As a trail guide in Hluhluwe-iMfolozi Park, his office is 100,000 hectares of wilderness, and that's a lot of living system to love.

From our first meeting at Rhino Ridge Lodge I felt a kinship with Nunu, biophiliacs both of us. I found him in crisp khakis, checking his rifle. We're about the same height, and we speak the same language, near enough. His homeplace is in the borderlands of KwaZulu-Natal, Mozambique and eSwatini, close to my own.

Nunu's motto is 'let your spirit meet the wilderness'. He doesn't just talk the talk, he walks the walk – and barefoot. He saw my surprise and laughed. Don't worry, he said, it's not compulsory. It's something he likes to do, to feel the cool morning earth, the tickle of themeda grass, the river mud between his toes. Sometimes connecting with nature can be very physical.

With the sunrise warming our backs, we wandered into the bushveld. Within moments we had been absorbed, just two more beings moving in the landscape. We chatted freely, something I'm not used to doing when on foot. Won't we alarm the animals? Nunu explained that the normal rule for groups on trails is 'no talking while walking', and the main reason is that the guide is always listening to check for danger, so doesn't want any chatter behind. Today, with just two of us, he wants the animals to notice that we are around, and not take them by surprise, so it's another style.

Nunu's point was proved a few minutes later: our first meeting with that armoured car of the veld, *Ceratotherium simum*, the southern white rhino. He was busy grazing, turning his head to look at us without pausing in his business. Totally calm, as if he was expecting us. He was at once strong and vulnerable – 133 of these magnificent animals were poached in KwaZulu-Natal in 2019. Nunu murmured greetings and good wishes, and we left him in peace.

My mind was on senseless death when I realised Nunu was telling a story about uMlahlankosi, the buffalo thorn we were standing beside. I'd heard it before, but every Zulu has their own way of explaining the tree's significance in afterlife transport, bringing spirits home to rest amidst the ancestors, to watch over the living. He carefully selected a branch, showing how the thorns are in pairs, one straight and a barbed one in the opposite direction: go wheresoever life is taking you, but don't forget about the people you left behind, take care of them. A message for both the living and the dead.

Those barbs of the buffalo thorn certainly have a way of making us slow down when exploring. It's another reason Nunu likes to go barefoot, forcing a pace that is kind to bare skin, and allows for slow discovery and sensory absorption. I fondled the pale green bark of a red ivory as Nunu extolled its wood. A tiny movement in the root system drew our eyes to the home of a trapdoor spider, a masterpiece of miniature engineering and camouflage.

Stopping to investigate a fresh aardvark excavation, I watched Nunu flick at a fat tick without annoyance. Even these little biters are a vital part of the ecosystem, food for those aardvarks, snakes and guineafowl. The diseases they carry play a role in naturally managing wildlife populations. The carcasses of these animals provide food for African wild dogs, hyenas and other scavengers, who in turn feed the ticks.

Markus Jungnickel

The white rhino turned his head to look at us without pausing in his business.

African wild dogs are often spotted in Hluhluwe.

The web of natural interdependence is endlessly fascinating, and is best appreciated by leaving the wheels behind for a morning. We followed the spoor of a genet until it was lost in the tracks of a pack of African wild dogs. Also known as 'painted wolves', these handsome animals are neither dog nor wolf, and are at risk of extinction, being on the endangered Red List of the International Union for Conservation of Nature. Entire packs have been lost in the park due to canine distemper, a viral disease which is spread easily through the sharing of food.

With the sun higher in the sky, we climbed back to Rhino Ridge Lodge, to a breakfast with a view. Hills in shades of brown and green faded into the haze to the south and east. Verdant thickets traced the river systems, the Hluhluwe flowing into the Umfolozi.

When it comes to conservation, size matters. A park with the scale of Hluhluwe-iMfolozi is big enough to allow wildlife systems to cope with natural setbacks and rebound. Setting aside land for conservation can mean rolling back some traditional human uses, such as stock grazing and hunting. Rhino Ridge Safari Lodge is built on community-owned land, with direct access to the Hluhluwe section of the park. Through job creation and concession licensing, it offers a sustainable commercial model for the community, and a win-win for nature.

Nunu Jobe knows that biophilia means recognising the human connections with nature, and the need for sustainable usage of land and nature's riches. In addition to guiding, he works with Rhino Ridge to give guests the opportunity to learn about the Zulu people's interdependence with the natural world. Aside from walks to visit nearby communities, visitors can experience a homestay, and see how traditional and sustainable crafts are kept alive. It's a chance to take off your shoes and feel the natural energy of our wonderful earth. **HM**

The view from the deck at Rhino Ridge Safari Lodge takes in the distant hills.

Matthias Mullie/https://unsplash.com

With close to 100 mammal species, including rhino, and more than 350 bird species in Hluhluwe-iMfolozi Park, this park is rivalled only by Kruger National Park for species diversity.

Isibindi Africa Lodges

Leopard, along with other predators, range widely in the park, but are not easily observed. The best time for sighting a leopard is at night or in the early morning or late afternoon.

2 ▪ PHINDA PRIVATE GAME RESERVE

Giraffe and zebra graze in harmony in a lush landscape at Phinda Private Game Reserve.

Phinda Private Game Reserve shares its fenced northern boundary with uMkhuze Game Reserve (see chapter 3). A walk in Phinda can be conveniently combined with a visit to Hluhluwe-iMfolozi Park (see chapter 1) or iSimangaliso Wetland Park. Established in 1990, the 28,555-hectare reserve is a fine example of how degraded farmland can be rewilded once it has been conserved. Today it is a luxury destination, part of the experiential travel company &Beyond, and is highly regarded for its conservation work and wide range of big game, including black and white rhino. Lion and cheetah have been reintroduced, and there is prolific birdlife with over 400 species recorded.

Phinda is accessed from the west via the N2 national road, a four-hour drive from Durban. Three lodges are in the western zone of the reserve, which is hilly, and another three are in the flatter area of sandveld and wetlands to the east. Day visits and self-drive are not permitted in the reserve.

WALKING IN PHINDA PRIVATE GAME RESERVE

Phinda is an enjoyable reserve for walks year-round, but the ideal time for a walking safari is between April and September when temperatures range from the low teens at night to the high 20s Celsius by day.

The reserve is strong on exclusive 'experiences' rather than mere luxury lodges and game drives. These include the chance to spend a romantic night camped under the stars, or taking part in planned conservation activities such as replacing tracking collars on rhinos and elephants – which sees guests accompanying a veterinarian to dart the animals from a helicopter.

Phinda is one of the few private reserves in South Africa that has a strong focus on walking safaris. Walks here are an opportunity to discover more about how the flora and fauna have recovered since the land use in the area was switched to conservation. Guests are encouraged to get out and enjoy the reserve on foot, and there is a flexible selection of activities available. Four of the lodges in the reserve – Rock Lodge and Mountain Lodge in the west, and Forest Lodge and Vlei Lodge in the east – offer guests one-hour nature trails all year round. Most visitors participate in these short walks, while others set out on four-hour excursions tracking black rhino on foot. An intensive walking safari package is offered for those keen to explore on foot.

Specialist Walking Safaris

Phinda Game Reserve offers a specialist walking safari for people staying a minimum of two nights. In keeping with the price tag, this is tailored to guests' wishes – walkers can stay out in the bush all day if they want to. Led by a ranger and a tracker, walks combine viewing of big game and birdwatching with searches for fossils, plants and invertebrates. Lion, leopard and cheetah are present in the reserve and may be tracked. In the east, the reserve has 1,000 hectares of Africa's remaining rare dry sand forest where it may be possible to spot the elusive suni.

Walk type	Day walk
Booking	www.andbeyond.com
Cost category	Over R6,000
Group size	2–6
Min. age	16
Season	January–December

Guests get a close-up view of the smaller creatures in Phinda's woodlands.

andBeyond.com

Denis Costello

An elevated boardwalk offers a magnificent view of uMkhuze's bird-rich forest.

In the heart of Maputaland, north of the Hluhluwe-iMfolozi Park, is the 40,000-hectare uMkhuze Game Reserve (also spelled Mkuze and Mkhuze). Although often overlooked in favour of the bigger neighbouring reserves, uMkhuze deserves a visit; it is close to the N2 national road, so can be included as a stopover when travelling between the Kruger area and the KwaZulu-Natal coast. The park entrance is a four-hour drive from Durban, and is accessed via a gravel road that is rough in some sections.

Established in 1912, uMkhuze is owned by Ezemvelo KZN Wildlife and operated as part of the iSimangaliso Wetland Park. The south-east of the reserve shares a fenced boundary with Phinda Private Game Reserve, and this area has extensive wetlands with superlative birdlife and several hides. Following a reintroduction programme that began in 2013, there are a small number of lions in the park, and the kuMasinga hide is a good place to spot them early in the morning. The reserve also hosts African wild dogs, leopard, cheetah, black and white rhino and elephant.

WALKING IN UMKHUZE GAME RESERVE

uMkhuze is at a slightly lower altitude than Hluhluwe-iMfolozi, so summer temperatures are a few degrees hotter, with average daily highs of 30°C. The best walking period is from April to September. In the wetter summer months the Fig Tree Walk in the reserve may be closed due to flooding.

In theory, uMkhuze operates dawn and afternoon walks; because of a shortfall of guides, only one walk, the Fig Tree Walk, operated by Ezemvelo KZN Wildlife, was offered at the time of writing. If afternoon walks are available, it would be feasible to join one of them as a day visitor, but it's better to plan an overnight stay and take a morning walk. Ezemvelo KZN Wildlife offers a choice of cottages and safari tents at the main camp of Mantuma, as well as accommodation at a couple of bush camps in the reserve.

Dawn walks start at 05:30 in winter (March to October) and 05:00 in summer (November to February) and last about three hours, including the drive to the starting point. Afternoon walks, when available, start at 16:00 in summer and 14:00 in winter. Walks should be booked and paid for at the Mantuma reception desk before 19:00 on the day before the walk. It's a good idea to phone in advance to check the availability of guides, and to double-check the meeting time at reception.

Trails officer Patrick Mathe leads the way through the forest of sycamore fig trees.

Fig Tree Walk

Walk type	Day walk
Booking	www.kznwildlife.com
Cost category	Under R1,500
Group size	2–8
Min. age	16, or 14 if accompanied
Season	January–December

The must-do walk in uMkhuze Game Reserve explores the sycamore fig tree forest, and a walk can be requested when making a booking. This riparian forest is ancient, with some specimen trees dated to over 900 years. The trails officer meets the walkers at a nominated spot at either the main Mantuma camp or one of the bush lodges, and the walk begins with a 40-minute journey by game-viewing vehicle to the parking area at Nsumo Pan. From there, the three-kilometre trail leads through woodland to a suspension bridge over the seasonal uMkhuze River. A highlight of the walk is accessing the canopy boardwalk, which is an excellent bird-spotting location – look out for the rare wattle-eyed flycatcher. As well as the fig trees, there are beautiful fever trees with their distinctive green-yellow bark. Use of mosquito repellent is recommended on this walk.

4 ▪ ITHALA GAME RESERVE

Denis Costello

Characterised by high hills and deep stream beds, Ithala offers spectacular views.

Ithala Game Reserve is an attractive park in the north of KwaZulu-Natal that feels off the beaten track. An Ezemvelo KZN Wildlife reserve, it spans 30,000 hectares of hilly terrain that falls steeply to the Phongola River. Although the road to the main camp is tarred, most of the reserve has gravel roads that are best explored with a high-clearance vehicle. The nearest supply towns are Pongola on the N2 national road, and Vryheid, both an hour's drive from the entrance.

Established in 1972, the reserve has rewilded former grazing land and restored wildlife populations almost wiped out by hunting and tsetse fly-borne disease. These days it is home to modest numbers of elephant, buffalo, black and white rhino, spotted and brown hyena, and it is perfect habitat for leopard. There are no lion, cheetah or African wild dogs present, and most visible are giraffe, zebra, blue wildebeest, eland and other plains game. Like the other reserves of northern KwaZulu-Natal, the birdlife is prolific, and over 300 species have been recorded at Ithala.

Most accommodation is at the well-managed Ntshondwe Resort, which is very nicely situated amidst ancient boulders, acacias, wild figs and cabbage trees at the foot of the Ngotshe Mountain. The camp has a couple of short self-guided trails leading to lookouts, which are highly recommended. There are also a few bush camps and a campsite.

WALKING IN ITHALA GAME RESERVE

The late autumn and winter months from April to September offer the best walking conditions in northern KwaZulu-Natal, as summers are hot and humid. Midwinter mornings are chilly in an open vehicle, so walkers will need warm clothes until reaching the walk starting points; these can then be left in the vehicle.

With a mix of steep slopes and grassy plateaus, and the backdrop of the escarpment, a scatter of boulders and eroded rock formations, Ithala is a pleasant reserve for walking. For most of the year, the vegetation of grasslands and woody shrubs is not dense. Unusually for a reserve with big game, Ithala has a number of marked self-guide trails, most of which start at Ntshondwe Resort, with a steep climb up Ngotshe. For insights into the park ecosystem, the day walks led by Ezemvelo KZN Wildlife guides are recommended, with both morning and afternoon walks available. Ticks can be found in Ithala at any time of year, so it's advisable to wear long pants and sleeves or use insect repellent on bare skin.

Day walks

Dawn walks start at 07:00 in winter (from the beginning of March to the end of October) and 06:00 in summer, and afternoon walks start at 14:00 in winter and 15:00 in summer. They last about three hours, including the drive to the start. Walks should be booked and paid for at Ntshondwe Resort reception before 19:00 on the previous day.

As with most day walks operated by Ezemvelo KZN Wildlife, a single trail guide leads the walk. There are no lion present, and there is a low likelihood of unplanned encounters with elephant or buffalo on foot in the areas walked. It's possible to start walking directly from the resort, but more usual for the guide to travel in the guests' vehicle and start elsewhere in the reserve. There are a couple of favoured locations, one of which is close to the reserve entrance, and the trail guide will consult with the guests on where to go.

■ Walk type	Day walk
■ Booking	www.kznwildlife.com
■ Cost category	Under R1,500
■ Group size	2–8
■ Min. age	12
■ Season	January–December

Ezemvelo KZN Wildlife

Field guide Leonard Gumede eyes a white rhino.

EcoTraining

The pans and rivers of the Kruger National Park are the focus of many wilderness trails.

One of the world's great wilderness areas, the Kruger National Park is vast and straddles the eastern parts of the Limpopo and Mpumalanga provinces in the lowveld, bordering Mozambique and Zimbabwe. Established as the Sabie Game Reserve in 1898, the park has expanded to almost two million hectares and is surrounded by further protected lands to the west, north and east that cooperate internationally as the Great Limpopo Transfrontier Park (see the box on the Russian dolls of Limpopo on pages 122–123).

The variety of ecozones in the park, from mountain bushveld to mopane scrubland, savannah and riparian forest, make it a rewarding place for repeat visits. It is home to the full spectrum of southern African wildlife, including over 500 species of bird and some 1,600 lion – about half of all the remaining wild lion population left in South Africa.

Due to a combination of its accessibility and its rich ecosystem, the southern half of the park, between the Olifants and Crocodile rivers, has the highest density of walking safari opportunities in Africa. (In 2005, the name of the Olifants River was changed to Lepelle and that of the Crocodile River to Mgwenya; however, SANParks still uses the older names, a convention followed in this chapter.) As well as having better vegetation and a greater density of wildlife than the northern parts of the park, the south has far more camps and private lodges, and good access by road and air.

The central zone of the park, accessed via Orpen Gate, is less intensively visited, but contains some of its best-loved rest camps and private lodges, located close to the Timbavati and Sweni rivers. The dominant vegetation is knob thorn savannah and mixed bushwillow woodlands. The park's eastern frontier with Mozambique is marked by the volcanic Lebombo Mountains, which rise to almost 500 metres. The more open vegetation in the central Kruger Park attracts large numbers of herbivores such as impala, blue wildebeest and zebra – and their predators.

The northern areas of the park are drier, with poorer soils and smaller game numbers than the south. The Tropic of Capricorn crosses the park between Mopani and Shingwedzi rest camps, and in the subtropical zone the landscape takes on a different tinge, with a transition to tropical vegetation including baobab trees, and the appearance of birds such as the tropical boubou, Meves's long-tailed starling and the racket-tailed roller. The north has much less tourism infrastructure and receives fewer visitors. For this reason, many people prefer it to the south, and it has some excellent walking options.

The southern park gates are all four to five hours' drive from Johannesburg, while the central Orpen Gate is closer to six hours away. The northern half of the park is accessed via Phalaborwa, Punda Maria and Pafuri gates, all of them six to seven hours' drive from Johannesburg.

The best scheduled air connections and car rental options are at Kruger Mpumalanga International Airport, near Mbombela (Nelspruit). There are also domestic connections from Cape Town and Johannesburg to Skukuza, the largest rest camp in the park, which has its own airport.

WALKING IN THE KRUGER NATIONAL PARK

The Kruger National Park is the premier walking safari destination in Africa, and each year thousands of visitors enjoy the adventure of exploring its wilderness on foot. The park has dozens of places to start a day walk, including the park rest camps, bushveld camps, gates and private lodges. In addition, there are intensive walking safaris based at wilderness trail camps and specialist private trail camps, as well as backpacking trails.

The park is in the lowveld and has a hot, semi-arid climate. Throughout the park, walking is preferable in the cooler, drier months, ideally from May to September, although

Seolo Africa

There are over 17,000 elephants in the Kruger, and meeting some on a walking trail is not unusual.

Joe James

Guests on the Napi Wilderness Trail examine the remains of a buffalo.

in the midwinter months of June to August it can be chilly to sit outside in the evenings. The summer period from October to March is hotter and more humid, with temperatures exceeding 30°C. There is an increased likelihood of rainfall at this time, which usually comes in showers or thunderstorms. If rains have been good, the grass is longer, and there is a higher risk of ticks and mosquitos. It's noticeably hotter and drier in the north of the park. There, many migratory birds arrive in summer, and some stay into the autumn, making April and May top months to visit. The lowveld area is a year-round malaria risk zone, and visitors should take medical advice before travelling.

Day walks operate throughout the park all year long, and SANParks wilderness trails take just a short break around Christmas. Any seasonal fly camps run by private operators are taken down during the summer months, a time when the SANParks backpacking trails also stop.

From a walking perspective there is no 'best' area to visit, although it can be said that the south-west, far north and north-west have the most interesting terrain. The underlying geology determines the vegetation type and thus the fauna of each area, so the trail experiences vary from north to south – a distance spanning over 300 kilometres. The south-western zone between Malelane and Paul Kruger gates is mainly granite hills, and it has the best and deepest soils with vegetation classed as sourveld and mountain bushveld. Three of the SANParks wilderness trails are clustered in this zone, as well as the Jock Safari Lodge private concession.

As the landscape falls gradually to the east, the geology changes to basalts. Soils become much shallower east of the H1 tarred road, and the change in vegetation is noticeable. The upper Sabie River area close to the park headquarters at Skukuza Rest Camp is the locus of excellent walking experiences operated by Rhino Walking Safaris and the SANParks Honorary Rangers (SHR).

In this central part of the park, accessed via Orpen Gate, other walking safari options are the SANParks Sweni Wilderness Trail and the day walks operated by the luxury private Singita Sweni Lodge, both east of Satara Rest Camp near the Mozambique border.

From the Olifants River northwards the distinctive vegetation is mopane woodlands and shrubland. These hardy trees survive arid conditions and elephant grazing, but don't make for interesting walking. Happily, the north is crossed by a number of perennial rivers including the Olifants, Letaba and Luvuvhu, and bordered to the north by the Limpopo River. These and other seasonal watercourses nourish riparian woodlands and attract a huge number of bird species, and are the focus for SANParks's three adventurous backpacking trails. Although this area has less game capacity than the south, the concentrations near water sources result in good viewing, and the north is known for its large elephant population; buffalo and nyala are also common.

In the far north, the landscape becomes more interesting, and the Pafuri region features sandstone gorges, fever tree forests and dense populations of bird and animal life. Here you can find excellent walking on the SANParks Nyalaland Wilderness Trail and at the RETURNAfrica properties in the Pafuri Triangle, between the Luvuvhu and Limpopo rivers.

SANPARKS WALK EXPERIENCES

The vast majority of walking experiences in the Kruger National Park are offered by SANParks, with an impressive range of options that span day walks, wilderness trails and backpacking trails.

Wilderness trails from dedicated camps began in 1978 and, once their popularity was evident, walks from rest camps followed in 1991. Originally these walks started directly from the camps, but soon additional game-viewing vehicles were brought in so that walkers could start from different locations each day, which added variety to the experience while minimising the ecological impact of the walks. Today, dawn walks are available daily and year-round at all SANParks rest camps and bushveld camps. In addition, afternoon walks are offered at Skukuza and Letaba rest camps and, uniquely, Olifants Rest Camp runs a midmorning walk. To meet demand, new SANParks wilderness trails have gradually been added and there are now seven spread through the park. In the northern half of the park SANParks operates three backpacking trails, each centred on a different river system.

Generally, booking SANParks walks is easy once armed with the right information (see the box on booking on SANParks.org on pages 78–79). Bookings can be made almost a year in advance, with bookings for the 11th month opened on the first working day of each new month. For example, to make a reservation for June next year, bookings open on the first working day of July this year. Wilderness trails in particular are very popular and should be booked well in advance of planned travel. Bookings for walks are possible via the SANParks website, email, phone, or directly at the reception desk at rest camps. Wilderness and backpacking trail reservations are handled by an always helpful dedicated team. There are some walks that can only be booked by phone, but for most the website at sanparks.org is the most convenient booking channel.

With the shell of a giant African land snail in his hands, Guide Elliot Nkuna explains its habits on a dawn walk.

BOOKING ON SANPARKS.ORG

Walks in the Kruger National Park can be booked online via the SANParks website – unlike for other national parks. The following steps help to make sense of the online booking process for walks and trails in the park.

LOOK

It is possible to check for dates with availability without registration or sign-in on the SANParks website. Navigate to the Kruger National Park section. For camp accommodation bookings, look for the 'Availability: Accommodation' section. For walks, look for the 'Availability: Activities' section. **Note** that Backpacking Trail availability is included in the Wilderness Trail availability document.

SIGN IN

When you are ready to make an online booking, you need to sign in to your SANParks account. To create an account, registration is free and your passport details or a South African ID will be needed to complete the process. During the registration process, you will receive a client code, and you can use this for all future bookings with SANParks, online or not.

BOOK

DAY WALKS	OVERNIGHT TRAILS
■ Day walks are listed as a 'Single Day Activity'. ■ To book walks from rest camps, you must first book overnight accommodation in the relevant camp: book for the previous night for dawn walks, and for the subsequent night for afternoon walks. ■ Use the booking utility to check dates when both accommodation and walks are available at your desired camp(s), and create your shopping basket.	■ Wilderness and backpacking trails are listed as an 'Overnight Activity'. ■ These trails must be booked and paid for as a separate transaction to any other accommodation and activities you are booking. ■ All SANParks trails are 'open' – this means a group booking is not mandatory, and the trail can be shared with new friends. ■ Wilderness trails must be booked per two-bed unit. The trail tariff includes transport, accommodation, food and water, and the services of two guides and a cook. ■ Backpacking trail tariffs include transport and the services of two guides. ■ Use the booking utility to browse available dates and create your shopping basket.

CHECKOUT

● Online bookings must be paid in full at the time of booking.
● Booking online has the benefit of giving you a 5% discount for accommodation bookings, which sadly does not apply to walks.

CHANGES

Subject to availability, you can make changes to your booking without paying an extra fee up to your date of arrival.

It's possible to cancel a booking without penalty up to 30 days before the booked date. After that there are graduated charges for cancellations. Refunds will be held on your account for future bookings, or by request will be returned to you by bank transfer or to credit cards.

EMAIL AND PHONE BOOKINGS

The advantage of booking by phone or email is that it's possible to make reservations and pay later. A deposit of 33% must be paid within 30 days to keep the booking, with the balance to be paid in full 30 days before your date of arrival. The disadvantage is missing out on the 5% discount for booking accommodation online.

After completing a booking by phone or email, you'll be issued with an email reservation letter containing a Client Code and Reservation Reference. The most convenient way to pay is to use a credit card via the Quick Pay utility on the website.

If you're booking by email, consider using the website Request Form instead, to ensure that you submit all the necessary information. Registration is not required. You can find the form on the sanparks.org website under 'Booking Methods'. When you complete and submit the form, an email is automatically sent to the reservations office.

THE EXCEPTIONS

At the time of writing it was not possible to book online for walks from Crocodile Bridge, Shingwedzi and Punda Maria rest camps, bushveld camps, and the park gates. These walks must be booked by telephone via the following numbers:

- Bateleur Bushveld Camp: +27 (0) 13 735 6843
- Crocodile Bridge: +27 (0) 13 735 6012
- Malelane: +27 (0) 13 735 6152
- Numbi Gate: +27 (0) 13 735 5133; Cell: (0) 64 750 2318
- Orpen Gate – phone Orpen Camp: +27 (0) 13 735 6355/5127
- Paul Kruger Gate: +27 (0) 13 735 5107; Cell: (0) 64 750 2321
- Phabeni Gate: +27 (0) 13 735 5890; Cell: (0) 64 750 2322
- Phalaborwa Gate: +27 (0) 13 735 3547
- Punda Maria Gate: +27 (0) 13 735 6873
- Shimuwini Bushveld Camp: +27 (0) 13 735 6683
- Shingwedzi Rest Camp: +27 (0) 13 735 6806/7
- Sirheni Bushveld Camp: +27 (0) 13 735 6860
- Talamati Bushveld Camp: +27 (0) 13 735 6343

Walks from rest camps

A dawn walk can be the most memorable experience of a visit to South Africa's greatest park, and it would be a shame to stay in the Kruger Park and not venture on at least one. These walks can be enjoyed by both the bushwalking enthusiast and those for whom it's a rare adventure. The pace is always on the gentle side, the distance modest, and the guides tend to avoid inclines and river crossings.

▦ Walk type	Day walk
▦ Booking	www.sanparks.org
▦ Cost category	Under R1,500
▦ Group size	4–8
▦ Min. age	12
▦ Season	January–December

There is no preference of camp to choose for walks, but rest camps are more likely than bushveld camps to have the required minimum number of walkers and guide availability. If you've reserved a walking activity in advance – and you should – then let the reception staff know when you check in at the camp, so that they can make sure your name is on the list, pick up the indemnity form, and note the walk meeting place and time. At the rest camps, even if you don't have an advance booking, it may be possible to join a walk if there's space. Just enquire at the camp reception.

As the walks start early, hikers must have accommodation booked in the camp the night before. It will be dark when you meet to start the walk, so bring a torch for the walk from the accommodation to the meeting area.

Walks start with a slow drive in an open-sided game-viewing vehicle, and for chilly mornings the vehicles usually have blankets on board. Driving from the camp allows the walk to begin in a new place each day, and reduces the impact on the environment of repeated human intrusion. Walkers are unlikely to see other human footprints.

Routes vary daily to reduce the impact on the environment.

The lead guide adjusts the pace and distance of walks to suit the group, and a typical dawn walk will cover four to six kilometres over three hours. That leaves plenty of time to stop for short talks about nature given by the lead guide. There is one longer rest stop for snacks and drinks, which are included in the cost and carried by the guides to share with the group.

While dawn is the preferred time of day to go out on a walk, Skukuza and Letaba rest camps also run afternoon walks. An overnight booking at the relevant rest camp is required, as they return to camp at (or even after) gate-closing time.

Uniquely, Olifants Rest Camp offers a two-hour river walk that starts at 09:00 in summer and 09:30 in winter. This is the only walk that is deep in the park and accessible to day visitors. Participants should enter the park via Phalaborwa Gate as soon as it opens at 05:30 (06:00 from April to September), to allow three hours for the drive to Olifants.

Getting out early on a dawn walk rewards walkers and photographers with the richest light.

Joe James

SANPARKS DAY WALK MEETING TIMES

Day walk type	Summer: 1 October–31 March	Winter:1 April–30 September	Duration
Dawn walks	04:00	05:00	3 hours
Afternoon walks	16:00	15:30	2.5 hours
Olifants River walk	09:00	09:30	2 hours

Walks from park gates

It's not necessary to stay in the Kruger National Park itself to avail yourself of SANParks day walks. There are numerous private lodges close to the south and central park gates, and it's possible to book walks that meet at these gates. SANParks trail guides lead the walks, and the experience is the same as for walks from SANParks rest camps. Afternoon walks from these gates are also sometimes possible, depending on the number of walkers and guide availability.

▦ Walk type	Day walk
▦ Booking	www.sanparks.org
▦ Cost category	Under R1,500
▦ Group size	4–8
▦ Min. age	12
▦ Season	January–December

The gate walks are not publicised by SANParks, as they appear to exist to accommodate private lodges and safari operators. The easiest way to book gate walks is to make a request via a lodge or travel agent, but individuals can book by phone with the gate or nearest rest camp. When they make a booking, walkers are given instructions on the meeting place. A game-viewing vehicle will rendezvous with them at the gate, and return them to the same spot after the walk. As walkers don't formally check into the park, they are exempt from the daily conservation fee. Guests who wish to drive into the park after the walk just check in as usual at the gate, and pay the fee or show their Wild Card.

Apart from the different booking method involved, gate walks are the same experience as camp-based walks and have the same departure times, duration and other conditions.

Rhino tracks and elephant snacks

Not long after passing through the Kruger National Park's Phabeni Gate, I was following a little white hatchback when suddenly its brake lights lit up. I stopped to check their discovery – and found a herd of impala staying cool in the shade of a thorn bush. As I manoeuvred to go around the car and continue on my way to Skukuza Rest Camp, I was reminded that everyone has a first time in Kruger, and that the novelty of that first glimpse of an animal in its natural habitat, even the common impala, endures. It's something that the best guides remember, too. It must be hard for them to always maintain their enthusiasm for sharing things that are mundane when working in the park.

Early the next morning, I was lucky to have Elliot Nkuna as a walking guide, finding him already in a laughing mood and keen to share his stories. This sort of guide realises that a guest can be fighting jet lag, and even be a little apprehensive about going on foot among the wildlife. Elliot takes a guest's nervous excitement and builds on it. He knows people like the thrill of close encounters with big animals, but must also be prepared for their failure to appear.

But that morning, the wildlife played its part – and in plenty. As we drove to our starting point, we met a pack of African wild dogs hunting impala, sprinting past the feet of bemused giraffes. Elliot is familiar with this pack, which tends to stick to its territory near Skukuza. After we had

Denis Costello

Guide Elliot Nkuna explains how elephants dig to access water in riverbeds.

left the vehicle and set off in silent single file, the sightings came one by one: a lone hyena, a little family of dwarf mongooses, a skittish steenbok, a white-backed vulture on its nest of sturdy branches high in an acacia tree.

Between encounters, Elliot made sure we were never bored by stopping for micro-classes in nature. He showed us chalky white hyena droppings, explaining how to tell them apart from crocodile dung, which looks similar. Other animals, including tortoises, will eat these droppings to access the calcium they contain, a little link in the endless cycle of nature.

Elliot examines tracks found on the trail.

We found many trees knocked over, roots exposed and recently chewed. After an hour we met the culprit, a large bull elephant. Elephants love the nutrient-rich roots. And I love elephants, but I value trees too, and it's a shame to see a 50-year-old thorn tree toppled for a snack. He soon spotted our group and threw his ears forward, swung a front leg and gave us a stare. Time for us to move on.

The best was yet to come, as Elliot gave us an exquisite lesson in tracking. Stopping to show us some rhino prints, he first explained how we could recognise them as those of white rhino and not its rarer black rhino cousin. Then he stood with the prints between him and the sun to get the best angle of light. He pointed out the sharply defined edges of the indentation in soft sand, and the colour change where the darker sand had been exposed. 'This track is very, very fresh,' he said. We moved on, keeping silent. In just a few minutes, as if by prior arrangement, we found her. She was busy in a dry riverbed, excavating a drinking hole. Something alerted her to our presence – a scent or sound – and she jolted and trotted up the river bank. She stopped to turn and look, then moved on, understandably grumpy. We investigated the waterhole. It would first have been dug by an elephant, using its feet and trunk. Elephants prefer not to drink from stagnant pools, and the sand filters clean water for their needs – up to 200 litres per day for an adult.

We looped back to the vehicle, a happy bunch. On the return drive, we didn't stop to view the impala. I chatted with an American honeymooner, thrilled with his first experience of the African wilds. His bride was not well, and had stayed in camp, and he was wondering how to diplomatically tell her what she'd missed. We agreed that the best thing was to plan another walk for them to share. **HM**

Of all the walking options covered in this guide, the SANParks Wilderness Trails rank near the top in terms of experience and value for money, and are highly recommended. Each trail takes adventurers into the wild for three nights to stay at a fixed camp, fully catered and accessed by private roads.

There are seven SANParks wilderness trails in the Kruger National Park (described in the following pages), and they all have the same format; it isn't possible to book for shorter or longer stays than the standard three nights. Apart from short summer breaks for maintenance, they run year-round, with departures on Wednesdays and Sundays. There is a discount in the hotter months from 1 November to 28 February. They are very popular and it can be hard to get a booking. Don't fret about which trail to book, as all offer an excellent experience.

The trails are run from special permanent camps that are protected from large animals by unobtrusive electric fences. Walkers stay together as a group for the three nights, with walks in the morning, some rest time during the day, and another walk or drive in the afternoon. The roads to the wilderness camps are not accessible to other visitors, so whether on foot or in the vehicle, guests won't see any others than their group.

There's no electricity at the camps, just some solar power for room lighting and device-charging. In the evening, guests dine and relax by the light of a campfire and kerosene or solar lanterns. Apart from two camps with en-suite accommodation, they have shared ablutions with gas geyser showers and flush toilets. Drinking water, instant coffee and tea are provided at the camp, and fruit cordial in the morning. Guests can bring their own drinks to the camps, and shared gas-powered fridges are available. There's usually a good spot nearby to walk or drive to for a sundowner. In addition to two guides, each camp has a manager/cook, and the food is always of a good standard. A typical meal might be chicken casserole or a braai. Vegetarians or those with special dietary requirements should give advance notice of this, as South African cuisine is meaty.

Each wilderness trail has a nominated base camp, one of the SANParks public rest camps, where trail guests meet at 15:30 on the first day. On the final day, guests will be back at the base camp before lunchtime, so it's possible to do a wilderness trail without booking other accommodation in the park; but it's more relaxing to stay in the base rest camp the night before starting the

Joe James

Walkers on the Napi Wilderness Trail stop for a rest.

Leisurely afternoon walks may start from the trail camp or from a spot just a short drive away.

trail. Guests' vehicles remain at the base camp, and big suitcases may safely be left in the car, so participants can just bring what they will need for the three nights.

On the starting afternoon, guests and their guides travel by game-viewing vehicle to the wilderness trail camp, with stops to see wildlife. The game-viewing vehicle remains with the group for the duration of their stay. Each camp has four twin-accommodation units with two proper beds and mosquito nets. Four camps have thatched A-frame huts, while three have canvas tents on wooden decks.

In the evening the lead guide will deliver a briefing on the plan for the next day. Each morning of the two walking days, guests are woken about an hour before sunrise, and rise to have a hot drink and a rusk. Walks may start directly from the camp or, more typically, start with a short drive.

The walks last four to five hours, covering up to 15 kilometres. The guides carry a snack for breakfast – fruit, sausage or biltong, a packet of fruit juice. Back at camp, there's time for a wash before a late morning cooked breakfast, juice and cereals. Sometimes a drum is beaten to let everyone know when a meal is served, or when it's time for the afternoon walk. The afternoon walks are much shorter, and often involve driving to a good location to take a short stroll and sit and observe. Drives are mostly confined to restricted roads, with no other vehicles to be encountered.

Camps have a _lapa_ and camp chairs where walkers can relax in the shade. In the evenings the fire is the focus, a time for stargazing and chats, after which most trailists will retire by 21:00. In keeping with the wilderness spirit, excessive drinking of alcohol is strongly discouraged. On the fourth day there's no walk, so there's a slightly later wake-up call, and guests return to the base camp after breakfast.

Wolhuter Wilderness Trail

■ Walk type	Wilderness trail
■ Booking	www.sanparks.org
■ Cost category	R1,500–R3,000
■ Group size	4–8
■ Min. age	12
■ Season	January–December

Accommodation at Wolhuter Camp is in two-person A-frame huts.

Wolhuter was the first wilderness trail established in the Kruger National Park, and opened in July 1978 as a tented camp designed by Regional Ranger Mike English. As the first Head of Trails in the park, English can be thanked for having introduced wilderness trails. He was known for his fluency in Shangaan, one of the languages of the region, and was a San rock art expert.

The trail is named in memory of one of the first rangers, Harry Wolhuter (1877–1964), and the camp is in an area of mixed woodlands in the south-west of the park, in a subzone that is classed as a botanical reserve. The base camp is Berg-en-Dal, and the nearest gate is Malelane, about an hour's drive away. In 1986 it was upgraded with the present A-frame thatched huts, and is located under towering trees with a waterhole view. For many visitors the proximity of the waterhole is a highlight, providing day-long entertainment.

This area is perhaps the most scenic of the wilderness trails in the south, with granite outcrops, wooded valleys and areas of flatter bushveld. The walking can be a bit hilly, but walkers are rewarded with opportunities to sit atop koppies to practise 'sit and wait'-style wildlife spotting. There's a good chance of seeing white and black rhino, elephant and buffalo. The vegetation is classed as Malelane mountain bushveld, and supports a proliferation of game including blue wildebeest, mountain reedbuck, zebra, giraffe and kudu. There are also San rock art and Iron Age archaeological sites to be explored.

Stolsnekdam and Mangake Hill are photogenic features of the Wolhuter Wilderness Trail area.

Bushmans Wilderness Trail

■ Walk type		Wilderness trail
■ Booking		www.sanparks.org
■ Cost category		R1,500–R3,000
■ Group size		4–8
■ Min. age		12
■ Season		January–December

Bushmans Wilderness Trail camp is five kilometres distant from Wolhuter camp and is located in similar hilly terrain. The walking is in mountain bushveld, often with a climb to a rocky lookout to sit and observe, but the highlight of this trail is the chance to see 25,000-year-old San rock paintings.

The camp is in a beautiful location, nestled among granite hills. It has operated at this site since July 1983. Following refurbishment in 2020 it now has tented units with en-suite facilities.

The wildlife is similar to that on the Wolhuter Trail – there's a good chance of finding rhino, while elephant, buffalo, kudu, klipspringer and mountain reedbuck are commonly spotted. Nightfall brings the sounds of the freckled nightjar and spotted eagle owl. As with the Wolhuter Trail, the base camp is Berg-en-Dal, which is a one-hour drive from the nearest gate at Malelane.

Napi Wilderness Trail

■ Walk type		Wilderness trail
■ Booking		www.sanparks.org
■ Cost category		R1,500–R3,000
■ Group size		4–8
■ Min. age		12
■ Season		January–December

The evening campfire is the venue for reminiscing about the day.

The Napi Trail terrain is less hilly than the other trails in the southern section of the park. Nevertheless, it is interesting walking territory, with granite underlying mountain sourveld and broadleaf woodland in the catchment of the Napi and Bimyati rivers. There are several seasonal pans that draw wildlife, and it's a good area for spotting rhino and even lion. The Bimyati drainage line is the focus for birdwatching, and the area is known for the presence of the thick-billed cuckoo, which lays its eggs in the nests of Retz's helmetshrikes.

Camp accommodation is in canvas tents on wooden decks. It is regarded as a more comfortable camp as it's one of just two wilderness trail camps that offers en-suite facilities. The camp opened in October 1991, and had a full makeover in 2018. Pretoriuskop is the base camp for the trail, and the nearest gate is Numbi Gate, 20 minutes away.

On the trail of lions

Ahead of the game-viewing vehicle, an alarmed black mamba catapulted itself from the roadway into the dry grass. We stopped to see if we could get a closer look, but our eyes were diverted upwards to the treetops, where a score of vultures perched in their 'hands-in-pockets' style. We didn't need the guides to tell us there was a carcass nearby, but the bush was impenetrable. What followed showed the difference between a regular game drive and the experience of a wilderness trail.

Our group was on the second day of the Napi Wilderness Trail. We'd spent the morning on foot in a remote corner of south-west Kruger National Park, and now we were taking it easy with an afternoon drive on a restricted, unsurfaced road, heading for Transport Dam. Under normal circumstances we'd have peered into the greenery for a while before moving on. But now Calsi, our guide, simply said 'let's have a look', and told us to get down and follow him and his assistant guide, Philemon. We were set for an adventure. Warned to be quiet, we crept behind them, keeping an eye out for the black mamba. After a few moments we heard a distinct growl that made everyone jump. The guides reversed towards us – lions ahead near their kill. The cats had seen the guide and dashed away.

We retreated, excited to be on foot and so close to the big cats. Back in the vehicle, we drove a couple of hundred metres and then got out to follow Calsi into the bush again. I wondered how he knew which way to go, and later he told me he could hear the lions, as they use a low cough to communicate with their young. Incredibly, he led us directly to the pride of seven, now relaxing and well fed. For a minute or two, we had a 50-metre staring contest. Then one of the males stood and started flicking his tail, glancing at his comrades as if to say: 'Are you with me?' Calsi immediately had our group in a steady reverse and soon safely back to the vehicle.

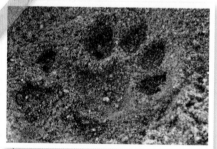

Joe James

Joe James

The thrill of tracking lion on foot was the highlight of our wilderness trail experience.

The encounter encapsulated the serendipity of the wilderness trails experience. The morning walk had been less dramatic, but no less interesting. We'd spent half an hour simply sitting watching two tortoises battling. Calsi and Philemon had an endless trove of nature's wonders to share – the nest of a weaver bird, flowering plants, a dung beetle at work. It was early February, and a couple of hours after sunrise the temperature reached 32°C, so we took frequent rests, snacking on bananas and biltong. After 4.5 hours of walking we returned to the trail camp to find a pair of elephants in the river below. It seemed a shame to sleep when there was so much to see, but the early start and tiring walk made a midday nap irresistible.

Joe James

Our Napi Trail camp had canvas tents on wooden decks, with en-suite facilities.

The camp is fenced, but it only keeps out the big animals. In a hollow under one of the few rough wooden steps on the sloping track to our tent we found a plump puff adder at rest, a good reminder to use a torch after dark. It also made us appreciate the camp's en-suite facilities. Unlike most snakes, puff adders are known to stand their ground rather than head for the long grass. We gave this one its space, and it remained there for the whole of our stay.

We didn't think that the third day on the trail could live up to the excitement of the previous day – but we were wrong. The walk was just as interesting. We came face to face with a baby giraffe, which seemed just as fascinated by humans as we were with it. Kudu were less curious, darting into bush cover, while wildebeest turned tail in a cloud of dust. The breakfast break was taken sitting on smooth boulders in a riverbed. A sound made Calsi curious – he went a little distance away to check and found the tracks of a pair of leopards, but they eluded our attempts to spot them. We moved on, finding a black rhino and its calf, and then surprising a hyena in some long grass. This area of Kruger is known for its density of wildlife, and did not disappoint.

After the siesta at camp, it was time to venture out again by vehicle. With the temperature by now in the mid-30s, we were happy there was no suggestion of another walk. We drove to the tarred H2-2 road and followed it west a little before turning north onto a restricted road. Calsi had seen other lions in this area the previous week and knew there was a good chance they were still close by. We arrived to find a huge male lying on the track, his female in the grass nearby. They were taking a break from mating, but soon continued, not at all bothered by the vehicle close by. Calsi explained that the mating lasts for days, with the cats coupling hundreds of times.

With darkness falling, we reversed our route. During an interlude with wheels spinning in a deep sandy gully, we spotted a white-tailed mongoose setting out for a night of feeding. This was our first wilderness trail in the Kruger, and quite different to what we had imagined. The camp was a lot more comfortable than anticipated, the food top class. The walking was less than expected, but plenty given the heat. The biggest surprise was the evening drives, when we had the best animal encounters, and in areas away from public access; just as good as the finest private safari locations that cost five times more.

On the fourth day, there was the luxury of a longer lie-in until 05:30 before departing for Pretoriuskop Rest Camp. Even then, the wildlife viewing continued, with a 200-strong buffalo herd on the road – the one big animal we'd not encountered on foot. **DC**

Joe James

Napi Camp has a hide on its boundary, perfect for spying on the waterhole between walks.

Sweni Wilderness Trail

■ Walk type	Wilderness trail
■ Booking	www.sanparks.org
■ Cost category	R1,500–R3,000
■ Group size	4–8
■ Min. age	12
■ Season	January–December

Joe James

The waterhole viewed from Sweni Camp.

Sweni Wilderness Trail is in the central Kruger National Park, in a basalt area of grassy plains and thorny savannah. Here it's harder for the wildlife to hide than in the thicker bush to the south, so it's possible to tick off quite a few species. The themeda grasslands support large herds of buffalo and antelope when feeding conditions are right, and these attract predators. As the terrain is pretty flat, it suits those averse to hill walks.

The camp has a waterhole, a pool in the Sweni spruit, so during the day guests can watch animals come to drink while enjoying a cold one of their own. It's not unusual to go to sleep to the sound of lions close by. The camp opened in October 1990, and accommodation is in thatched A-frame huts. The base camp for the trail is Satara Rest Camp, about an hour's drive away, and the nearest gate to Satara is Orpen, reached after a two-hour drive.

Mathikithi Wilderness Trail

■ Walk type	Wilderness trail
■ Booking	www.sanparks.org
■ Cost category	R1,500–R3,000
■ Group size	4–8
■ Min. age	12
■ Season	January–December

Joe James

The Mathikithi Trail takes walkers through a landscape of grasslands and woodlands.

Located on the banks of the N'wanetsi River, six kilometres south-west of Satara Rest Camp, Mathikithi is the newest trail and was established to replace the Metsi Metsi Trail, which closed in 2013 due to deterioration. A temporary fly camp called N'watinwambu was used until Mathikithi was established in 2015, with large tents on wooden decking. It is named after a 313-metre sandstone hill, 500 metres away from the camp, which is perfect for sunset views, and the mixed bushveld habitat is similar to that of Sweni. Walks are led in grasslands and riparian woodlands, and there are some lovely Natal mahogany trees for shady rests.

Some of the tents are exposed to the sun, which makes them hot for a midday siesta. The nearest gate to Satara is Orpen Gate, a two-hour drive. Take the opportunity by the campfire to ask the guides to tell the tale of a lion incident that occurred on the Metsi Metsi Trail in 2008.

Olifants Wilderness Trail

The Olifants Wilderness Trail camp is in the central sector of the Kruger National Park, amidst the low-rising Lebombo Mountains close to the border with Mozambique. Because the rivers here are perennial, there are often great concentrations of animals when it's dry in this region, and it makes for an entirely different experience to the wilderness trails in the south. The mixed terrain of flat open grasslands, river valleys and sections of forest means that each walk feels different. The confluence of the Letaba and Olifants rivers is about three kilometres downriver from the camp, and the river is busy with hippo, crocodile, fish eagles and waterbuck.

■ Walk type	Wilderness trail
■ Booking	www.sanparks.org
■ Cost category	R1,500–R3,000
■ Group size	4–8
■ Min. age	12
■ Season	January–December

Olifants is one of the oldest wilderness trail camps, running since November 1979, and is situated in a fine location overlooking the deep valley of the Olifants River. The camp huts are thatched A-frames with shared ablutions.

Getting to the starting point for the Olifants Wilderness Trail requires a longer journey than that to the five wilderness trails in the south of the park. The base camp is Letaba Rest Camp (beware, not Olifants Rest Camp), which is a two-hour drive from the nearest park gate at Phalaborwa. From Letaba the journey by game-viewing vehicle to the trail camp can take up to a further two hours, depending on stops.

Joe James

The Olifants River draws abundant game; both are top attractions of the Olifant Wilderness Trail.

KRUGER NATIONAL PARK ZONING

Kruger National Park visitors will notice many alluring unsurfaced vehicle trails with 'no entry' signs. Some of these lead to staff facilities, private concessions and bits of park infrastructure, but others are gateways to the large areas of the park where access is controlled under a designated zoning system.

The park zones, defined in the park management plan, are designed to conserve biodiversity while catering for tourism and leisure activities. There are five visitor-use zonal types: wilderness, remote, primitive, low-intensity leisure and high-intensity leisure. Over 80 per cent of the park falls into the first three zones and is thereby 'conservation-oriented', while the rest of the park is 'tourism-oriented'.

Walking safaris allow visitors to access parts of the park that vehicle-based visitors cannot reach. Under strict conditions, walks operate in the first three zones, while motor safaris are confined to the tourism zones. The most pristine 'wilderness' and 'remote' zones can only be accessed on foot. The areas zoned 'primitive' have no surfaced roads but allow for controlled low-volume activities, such as mountain-biking, horse riding and guided 4×4 adventure trails. As the SANParks and private wilderness trails are based in permanent camps that are serviced by unsurfaced roads, these camps are in the primitive zones. From the fixed camps, walkers penetrate into wilderness and remote zones on foot.

The Kruger Park is a revenue engine generating over R1 billion each year for SANParks, and at least the same again in spin-off benefits to the surrounding region. Yet there is constant pressure to find new ways to grow park income, especially as high-cost anti-poaching activity has expanded in recent years. New income sources can take the form of more luxury lodge concessions, 'pop-up' camps, or commercial adventure and entertainment events. Naturally, there is great resistance to developments that erode the wilderness, or to events that disturb the wildlife, especially from veteran park visitors.

Even walking tourism has an environmental impact on the park. Lodges and wilderness trail camps need 4×4 access, water supplies and sewage treatment. The latest plan for the park mentions the intention to develop just one additional wilderness trail, called Phambi. It is a delicate balance. The Kruger Park needs visitors in order to be self-sustaining and to survive, but too many would create a risk of damaging the very reason for its existence. At least by taking part in walking activities, visitors can enjoy the park while making a commercial contribution with minimal environment impact.

SANParks Wilderness Trail guests can access the most pristine zones in the park.

Nyalaland Wilderness Trail

The only SANParks wilderness trail in the far north of the Kruger National Park is Nyalaland (also spelled Njalaland). With gorges, sandstone koppies, rock art and baobabs, it's perfect walking territory. In fact, it was here that Regional Ranger Mike English proposed to establish the first Kruger wilderness trail in 1974, leading the Chief Director of the National Parks Board on a reconnaissance trip to the Lanner

■ Walk type	Wilderness trail
■ Booking	www.sanparks.org
■ Cost category	R1,500–R3,000
■ Group size	4–8
■ Min. age	12
■ Season	January–December

Gorge. Because of the war being waged in Mozambique at the time, and political unrest in Zimbabwe, the first trail was in fact the Wolhuter, located in the south of the park. That trail opened in 1978, and the Nyalaland trail camp followed in July 1980.

The camp was washed away in a flood in 2013, and was replaced by a temporary tented camp overlooking the Luvuvhu River. In 2018 it moved back to its original remote location at a bend in the Madzaringwe River, about a one-hour drive north of Punda Maria Rest Camp. Being so far from any tarred road, it has a wonderful air of remoteness. The view from the temporary location was better though, and it is likely that in the future a new wilderness trail will open on that site.

The habitat comprises rocky mopane savannah, deep sandstone gorges and riverine forest. It is a great area for birding, with the Pel's fishing owl and Verreaux's eagle owl local favourites. Other endemic species include the scarlet-chested sunbird, mottled spinetail, red-headed weaver and wattle-eyed flycatcher. Walkers will also probably see elephant, buffalo and nyala.

The trail offers an opportunity to view San rock art and Iron Age remains. One site with stone ruins is on a hilltop, seven kilometres from the camp. There are also dinosaur fossils to be found, and participation in the trail is the only way to reach them. Walks explore the Lanner Gorge, hyena caves and baobab forests, making this trail perhaps the most scenically interesting of all the wilderness trails. Bring a swimsuit, as the Luvuvhu River will be tempting on a hot day.

The camp accommodation is in thatched A-frame huts and ablutions are shared, with bucket showers suspended from a frame. Due to its location and the longer journey time to reach it, Nyalaland is the least heavily booked of the seven wilderness trails. The base camp is at Punda Maria Rest Camp, which is also the nearest gate, a seven-hour drive from Johannesburg.

The rich tree life is a feature of Nyalaland, as guide Jobe Shibangu explains.

Magriet Kruger

An encounter with an elephant is almost guaranteed on the
Nyalaland Wilderness Trail.

A hippo emerges from the Luvuvhu River.

The shy nyala may be spotted near water.

THE BACKPACKING TRAIL EXPERIENCE

A SANParks backpacking trail is the perfect choice for anyone who owns a hiking tent and camping stove. SANParks operates three backpacking trails in the northern half of the Kruger National Park, and they are the most demanding trails in the park: hikers carry everything needed for three nights of wild 'leave no trace' camping, and the reward is the chance to explore the deepest wilderness. The backpacking trails attract the most experienced and 'hard-core' trail guides, who have bottomless reserves of stories and bush knowledge.

The SANParks backpacking trails are generally similar to Ezemvelo KZN Wildlife's Primitive Trail in Hluhluwe-iMfolozi Park (see chapter 1), with a few differences. Here, hikers must supply their own kit and food, and everyone cooks for themselves. Hikers on the Primitive Trail sleep under the stars, whereas SANParks rules require that tents are used. Given the hot conditions, distances and sometimes small group sizes, it's regarded as too onerous for guides and guests to keep night watch.

All three backpacking trails are best accessed via Phalaborwa Gate, which is six hours from Johannesburg. Note that the shops in Kruger Park camps, while well stocked, are not geared to hikers. You should bring what you will need with you from home, or visit the big outdoor stores such as Cape Union Mart, Outdoor Warehouse or Trappers, all of which have outlets in the Highveld Mall near the N4/N12 junction in Emalahleni.

Backpacking trails begin on Sundays and Wednesdays only. Some guides establish a pre-trail WhatsApp group to pass on information and answer questions. The group and guides meet at a base rest camp for transfer to the trail by game-viewing vehicle, towing a trailer with the backpacks. The trail tariff covers transport between the base camp and the trailhead, and the guides' fees.

Hikers on backpacking trails need to be fit to carry a full backpack.

Backpacking trails are not endurance events and there are plenty of opportunities to take a rest.

Each backpacking trail explores a different river system, and the guides are careful to vary the start points, routes and camping spots, to reduce the impact on the environment and enhance the experience. There is flexibility to determine the plan of a specific trail based on the abilities and wishes of the hikers. The group may camp in a different place each night, or may stay in one camping spot for two of the three nights.

A good level of fitness is required, and hikers must be able to carry a full pack, often in full sun. It's important to understand that this is not trekking, and the goal is not to hike as far as possible. The daily walking distances vary from 10 to 15 kilometres, and, as with all other walks, there is plenty of time to stop and observe nature.

On a typical day, hikers are up before dawn to have breakfast and break camp. The group will be walking by 07:00, probably for four to five hours. If it's hot, the guides find a shady spot with a view to sit out the middle of the day. After another couple of hours' walking, guides and guests will confer to select a campsite, with enough daylight remaining to pitch tents and have a wash. Where there is a suitable river, the guides will find a safe spot to bathe. If there's no running river, it's feasible to have at least a 'cat wash' from whatever water source is available. Drinking water is sourced from nature, directly from a flowing river, or by digging a hole in the sand, elephant-style. Sand-filtered water may be safe to drink without any further purification, but check this with the guide.

In the evening it's sometimes possible to light a small fire, but all traces of it must be removed when breaking camp, including any firewood gathered and unused. On a clear night, far from artificial light sources, the star canopy is unbelievable. Tired hikers usually retire by 20:00 or 21:00. The night air is filled with the sounds of nature, and the tent fabric seems tissue-thin.

Olifants Backpacking Trail

■ Walk type	Backpacking trail
■ Booking	www.sanparks.org
■ Cost category	Under R1,500
■ Group size	4–8
■ Min. age	12
■ Season	April–October

Denis Costello

The Olifants Backpacking Trail closely follows the course of the river for most of the way.

Established in 2006, Olifants was the first SANParks backpacking trail and is regarded as the toughest, as it is the longest in terms of distance covered. The base camp is Olifants Rest Camp, and the trail has several variations, all exploring the catchment of the Olifants River between Olifants Rest Camp and the area where the river enters the park in the west.

The furthest trailhead, known as 'cul de sac', is over three hours' drive from Olifants Camp; hikers are driven back to Phalaborwa Gate and then south on a track inside the western boundary fence. From there it is a 45–50-kilometre walk to the usual pickup point at Wildevy, depending on the route. It's common to choose a more easterly trailhead and walk about 40 kilometres downriver. In any case, for most trail options there is a distance to cover, and the camp is moved each night.

Of the three backpacking trails, Olifants has the fewest variations, as the goal is to follow the river downstream. So the walking is mostly on the river levees, where there are splendid sycamore figs and marula trees for shady rests. The river is a wildlife magnet, with lots of hippo and elephant and prolific birdlife. From time to time, hikers will need to remove their footwear for river crossings, with the water usually deeper in the autumn months of April and May. There's a good selection of safe riverside camping spots, and an after-walk dip is generally possible. Although it's not obvious to the eye, the Olifants River is unfortunately polluted by phosphate mining and human settlements upriver, so water purification is essential.

There are shorter variations of the Olifants trail that start at tributaries of the Olifants River, the Tutsi River or the Shilondo River, and follow these to the Olifants River itself. From these start points it's feasible to spend the first night on the Olifants and then jump the watershed to the Hlaralumi River and spend a night there, and return to the Olifants for the third night. A rarer variation is to start at the usual end point at Wildevy and explore the river systems in that area. This makes the trail more like the Lonely Bull (see opposite page) and Mphongolo (see page 103) trails in style, and it's possible to camp for two nights in one spot and spend a day unencumbered by kit.

The trail participants meet at Olifants Rest Camp at 08:00 for departure at 09:00. The nearest gate to Olifants Camp is Phalaborwa, 3 hours 20 minutes away, so it's a challenge to stay outside the park and reach Olifants in good time, and preferable to arrange to stay in either Olifants or Letaba rest camps on the night before the trail starts. Typically, there are five to seven hours' walking on the second and third days, with shorter distances on the first and fourth. On the final day the group makes a rendezvous with the game-viewing vehicle by 10:00 for transfer back to Olifants Rest Camp.

The backpacking trail should not be confused with the Olifants Wilderness Trail (see page 92), which is a camp-based experience near the Mozambique border downriver from Olifants Rest Camp. The Olifants Backpacking Trail runs from the beginning of April to the end of October, with the best walking and bathing conditions likely from May to August. It has a shorter season than the other two backpacking trails because if summer rainfall is good, the waters rise too high to cross the Olifants River safely, making the trail unfeasibly long.

Lonely Bull Backpacking Trail

■ Walk type	Backpacking trail
■ Booking	www.sanparks.org
■ Cost category	Under R1,500
■ Group size	4–8
■ Min age	12
■ Season	February–November

Duncan Boustead

Sometimes Lonely Bull walkers venture further away from the river in search of a view.

Operating since early 2012, the Lonely Bull Backpacking Trail is the newest of the three backpacking trails and explores a wilderness area from the H14 Letaba low-water bridge eastwards to Mingerhout Dam. It can begin at several locations in the Letaba River area, or be accessed from the east where the Tsendze seasonal watercourse runs south and joins the Letaba.

Herds of hundreds of buffalo are spotted in this area, and hikers are sure to meet elephant, hippo and giraffe. There's a good chance of lion encounters. The trail is named after a favourite camping spot of game ranger Bruce Bryden, one shaded by Natal mahoganies. He named it for the lone buffalo and elephant bulls he'd found in the area on his first visits in the early 1970s.

There is no set route, and as there is no fixed distance to cover the guides will plan the hike based on the conditions, wildlife movements and the group's preferences. Some trails will break away from the river and delve deep into the mopane and bushwillow bushveld. The daily walking times are dependent on the heat and the group's abilities, and the trail is also suited to 'sit and wait'-style wildlife viewing.

By mid-afternoon, the guides will consult with guests to select a safe camping spot, and if this is close to the Letaba River there's the chance of a cooling afternoon dip when the flow is good. The group may decide to spend two nights at one camping spot, allowing for a day to explore the area without a heavy pack.

The base camp is Mopani Rest Camp and the nearest gate is Phalaborwa, a three-hour drive away. Lonely Bull's season runs from the start of February to the end of November, and there's a discounted trail fee in the heat of the first and last months of the season. With the extra effort required for backpacking, the trail is best tackled in the cooler winter months from May to August.

The blur of hoof and paw

The sands of the Letaba River bed are dappled with spoor and dung. Frankly, it's a mess. But our guide sees it differently. Piet van der Merwe scans the ground the way others read the news. This civet passed an hour or two ago on a dawn hunt. Here, a porcupine dragged its quills in the night. Beneath that dainty track, the unmistakable pads of a giraffe that came to drink yesterday evening. As Piet

Ready for another Letaba River crossing.

talks, my imagination wanders. Once, my ancestors might have walked this river bank, in what is now the Kruger National Park. They would have studied similar tracks with a life-or-death intensity, their well-being safeguarded by constantly reading their landscape.

For me, learning some of these skills from our guides would be the most fascinating aspect of the four-day experience. We were beginning the Lonely Bull Backpacking Trail, in the heart of South Africa's largest wildlife reserve. I set out with a mix of excitement and apprehension about the 'backpacking' part, with visions of toiling in the sun under a heavy load. But I need not have worried. Our guides measured their days in tales told, not kilometres walked.

We followed in silence, abiding by Rule One – 'When we walk, we don't talk'. But the Letaba is a highway of life, with endless reasons to stop and learn something new. I began to think that we had two guides not just for safety, but to share the storytelling duties. Duncan Boustead, the assistant guide, showed us a way to determine the number of people that had passed by a particular spot. Drawing two lines across the trail, a stride apart, he simply counted the footprints between the lines. Repeated at a few different points, this gives a very accurate tally, and is a technique used today when tracking poachers. We moved on a little, and Piet poked a chalky pile with a stick. 'Lion. Don't touch these by hand,' he warned. 'They can contain nasty stuff, worms and parasites.' He had no hesitation with herbivore droppings, picking them apart with his fingers to show us the clues that point to their owner. 'See these twigs, how they've been cut at an angle? Sure sign of black rhino.' He explained that their white rhino cousins are grass grazers rather than tree browsers.

Hang on – did you say lion? I turned to scan the low mopane forest that fringes the river. 'Yes, they're not far,' said Piet with enthusiasm. As the day was warming up, they'd probably retreated to a shady spot. For motorised visitors, this might be a typical lion sighting – a snoozing brown shape in the middle distance, perhaps the flick of a tail, half-hidden in the grass. For us, it was different, as on foot we could actively seek them out. Piet knew where to look, and we tentatively approached some dense bushes amidst the sandbanks. We found a perfect cat siesta spot, but there was nobody home, and perhaps that was for the best.

We set camp overlooking the river, picking a site behind an experimental fence, which detracted a little from the wild experience. The fence is designed to create an exclosure that allows small animals to pass freely, but blocks elephant and giraffe, and thus protects the trees. Huge nyala berry and forest mahogany flourish there. In eSwatini we call the latter tree umKhuhlu, and use the dried seeds to make beads.

With the sun low, we found a shallow and safe spot in the river to cool our bodies. Duncan perched on a rock, keeping watch over a herd of elephants, just in case. Our drinking water also came from the river, with purification drops added. After dark, as stoves boiled and fireflies danced, the stories continued. Other places, other trails. Close encounters and narrow escapes. Floods, droughts. Funny stories about treks past. I enjoyed the one about the guy with the enormous backpack, who carried everything possible. When the coffee was made, someone asked him for sugar, and he said, 'sure, white or brown?', producing a half kilo of each!

Washing off the day's sweat and dust in the river.

Denis Costello

I fell asleep to the sound of hippo squabbles. In the deepest dark, I woke to a rough cough – was that a lion? Next day, we were up before sunrise, eager to read the morning news in the sands. Less than 100 metres from the camp, we found more fresh lion spoor – they were tantalisingly close but out of sight. Duncan showed us a clever stratagem. Laying a stick between two prints, he took a measure of the stride and raised the stick vertically, indicating a point above waist high. 'That's his shoulder height – he's a big boy.'

Denis Costello

Some of the Letaba River crossings were tricky, and we took them slowly.

We took off our shoes, and followed Piet across the braids of the river, searching out shallow sections. Suddenly, an explosion of water caused him to jump back sharply – he'd almost stepped on a hippo hidden by reeds. Feeling a little faint, I followed him on a safe detour. Upriver, we were happy to sit for an hour within smelling distance of a pod of these grumpy beasts. Nearby, we watched a baboon trying to reach the nest of a Goliath heron that contained a single chick. He had second thoughts when the enormous bird stretched to its full height and wingspan.

Like everyone who has walked this river for aeons, we began to tune our senses to signs of danger. A great cloud of dust rising ahead was the first sign of a buffalo herd approaching for water. One hundred, then two, three hundred at least. A strong breeze carried our scent to a family of elephants, who raised their trunks to sniff with apprehension. 'They can't see us,' said Piet, 'and they don't know how far we are. But they know we are here.' They retreated, having learned that people can mean trouble, a huge bull taking up a defensive position behind his cows and calves. Definitely not the lonely bull.

By the last day, I'd stopped worrying about seeing lions or not. I was just happy to know they were out there, like the civet and porcupine, living their lives unbothered, less interested in us than we were in them. In a few days, our footprints would blur under hoof and paw, like those of all who had walked here before. Me, I'd happily reverse time and do it all again. **HM**

Mphongolo Backpacking Trail

■ Walk type	Backpacking trail
■ Booking	www.sanparks.org
■ Cost category	Under R1,500
■ Group size	4–8
■ Min. age	12
■ Season	February–November

The Mphongolo is the northernmost and 'wildest' of the three backpacking trails. It explores the largest section of designated wilderness in the park, an area of about 90,000 hectares between the Shingwedzi River in the south and its tributary the Mphongolo to the north. Between those two seasonal rivers are a number of other drainage lines that include the Phugwane (a tributary of the Mphongolo) and the Bububu, which joins the Shingwedzi near Shingwedzi Rest Camp. Mphongolo is a corruption of the name of a Venda chief, Mapongole.

The area's geology is mostly granite, with basalts to the east. It has a more varied landscape than the other backpacking trails, including open savannah, mopane woods, sodic pans and high gabbro koppies in the southern part. There are fine riverine woodlands, superior to those found on the more southerly backpacking trails, and beautiful baobabs. You can expect to see elephant, buffalo, black-backed jackal, wildebeest and antelope, and at least hear the sounds of lion and hyena.

In contrast to the Olifants and Lonely Bull backpacking trails, there's no perennial river on this trail, and the best chance to find rivers in flow is early in the season, from February to April. Depending on rainfall, pools can be found on the Mphongolo and lower Phugwane rivers, while the upper Phugwane and Bububu hold less water. There may be some distance between a campsite and a water source, so it's good to have at least four litres

Riverbeds are almost always dry in the Mphongolo area.

Hlengiwe Magagula

Digging for clean water in a spruit is hard work.

of container capacity. Drinking water is sourced by digging in the riverbed to reach the water table. Filtered through the sand, it can be consumed without chemical treatment, although it's safer to add some purification drops.

Mphongolo took its first paying guests in 2010, and originally the area was divided into nine blocks for trail purposes, extending to the western edge of the park. The block system is designed to reduce the environmental impact, and also to make it more interesting for repeat visitors. The lead guide and the section ranger decide which block each trail should explore, and return hikers can make contact with the guide in advance to request a specific area. It's best to ask not to walk too near the park's boundary, as the isolation of the trail can be spoiled by light and sound pollution from nearby settlements. Following years of drought, water is almost impossible to find in some blocks, so these zones are not walked often.

Areas of interest include the 400-metre-high Phonda Hills in the south-east of the walking zone, graves from the 1899–1902 South African War (formerly referred to as the Boer War) at Zati, and Matiyovia hot springs. As well as the baobabs, there are many standout jackalberry, wild fig and leadwood trees to be admired, and remnants of Iron Age settlements to be discovered. In recent years the park has embarked on a programme to remove man-made animal water sources, with a view to restoring the natural balance, and walkers may find disused windmills and decommissioned dams such as those at Wik-en-Weeg and Mooigesig.

The base camp for the trail is Shingwedzi Rest Camp, and the nearest gate is Punda Maria, almost three hours' drive from Shingwedzi. The trail meets at 12:00 for departure at 13:00. As with the Lonely Bull Trail, the season is from the start of February to the end of November, and there's a discounted tariff in the hottest months of February and November. May to August are the best months to walk the trail.

By sundown on day one, the trail camp is almost set and cooking will soon follow.

SANPARKS HONORARY RANGERS WALK EXPERIENCES

Visitors to the Kruger National Park and other SANParks reserves may meet friendly uniformed staff with 'SHR' badges. The wearer is a member of the SANParks Honorary Rangers volunteer corps, dedicated to working to help conserve the country's parks. The corps raises significant funds for SANParks, as well as providing unpaid labour such as clearing snares and invasive plants. It has a junior corps that educates youngsters in conservation through participation in field trips and workshops to learn about habitat, animals and plants, and how to identify and follow tracks.

Various local branches of the SHR take turns to fundraise by running wilderness trails in the Kruger Park. SANParks let them use the Bushmans and Wolhuter Wilderness Trail camps, usually in the hotter and less busy summer months. However, the majority of SHR trails operate from three camps that are exclusive to the organisation. Sand River Bush Camp, near Skukuza Rest Camp, and Nyarhi Rustic Bush Camp in the north are both ideal for a small group of friends or workmates. Mokhololo is a larger unfenced camp between Crocodile Bridge and Lower Sabie rest camps, made available to organisations for group bookings but not open to the general public. It's 300 metres from the Mokhololo Dam, which has a reputation as a powerful game magnet, drawing everything from elephant, buffalo and rhino to the kori bustard. The camp is fully catered, as it's designed for customer entertainment, team-building and staff motivation activities, and can accommodate up to 20 guests. It has hot showers and flush toilets, and guests sleep in two-person tents.

Despite not being marketed or bookable via SANParks channels, the SHR camps are heavily subscribed. The vibe is somewhat different to that of the SANParks-operated wilderness trails, with groups of friends and family returning annually, getting to know the Honorary Rangers, who always have a rich repertoire of stories to draw from, and who pitch in with the cooking. Dates for upcoming camps are advertised on the SHR website, and each is designed for a three-night stay. Group bookings are mandatory, with a fixed fee for up to eight guests. As with the SANParks wilderness trails, the idea is to spend as much time as possible on foot.

To take it to the extreme, the SHR runs South Africa's most adventurous walk, the Kruger Trail, which sees participants walking the entire length of the Kruger National Park.

Denis Costello

SANParks Honorary Ranger Francois van der Merwe explains how hippo incisors work.

A pause on the trail as the trail guide explains the science of termite mounds.

Faaiq Ebrahim Khan

Sand River Bush Camp

■ Walk type	Wilderness trail
■ Booking	www.sanparksvolunteers.org
■ Cost category	Under R1,500
■ Group size	6–8
■ Min. age	12
■ Season	March–October

The fenced Sand River Bush Camp is located not far from Skukuza Rest Camp in the Kruger National Park, near where the Sabie and Sand rivers meet, and there is a fine view over the Sand River from the camp. Guests meet the SHR volunteer guides at Skukuza Rest Camp, 30 minutes away from the nearest gate, Paul Kruger, before proceeding to the bush camp. Instructions on timing and what to bring are provided when you make your reservation.

Unlike on the SANParks wilderness trails, hikers can bring their own vehicles to the camp, as long as they have high clearance. There is no electricity, just some solar-powered lighting, and an emphasis on sustainable enjoyment of the wilderness.

Joe James

A .458 calibre bullet (almost 9cm long) is used to show the relative size of a lion paw print.

The camp tents are big enough to stand up in, and there are warm showers and flush toilets. Gas fridges, cooking utensils and braai facilities are provided. Guests must bring their own food and drinks, including drinking water, but kitchen utensils are supplied.

Walks take place in a similar terrain to those offered by Rhino Walking Safaris (see page 109), in mixed bushwillow savannah. It's not too hilly, as the trails explore the Sand and Sabie rivers and their riparian woodlands, which are full of birdlife. The area is rich in game and known for frequent lion sightings, and there's also a pack of African wild dogs in the locality. The walk duration is tuned to the wishes and abilities of the group, and can last from three to five hours. Motivated by their deep appreciation of all aspects of the bushveld, the Honorary Rangers make excellent guides. Shorter walks take place in the afternoon.

The Sand River Bush Camp is very popular, and it can be a challenge to get a reservation. To meet the demand, the SHRs are in the process of creating a 'Sand River 2' camp in the northern section of the park.

Nyarhi Rustic Bush Camp

Of all the camps in the Kruger National Park, Nyarhi Rustic Bush Camp, which has no fences or fixed tents, is closest in spirit to the famous wild camps of Botswana, known for their in-camp wildlife visitors. Nyarhi is designed to be booked by a single group of up to eight people. Each party stays in the camp for three nights, with daily bush walks led by Honorary Rangers. You can expect to go on up to six walks over the four days.

■ Walk type	Wilderness trail
■ Booking	www.sanparksvolunteers.org
■ Cost category	Under R1,500
■ Group size	6–8
■ Min. age	12
■ Season	March–October

The camp is set at a location near Fraser's Rest Waterhole, just off the Shongololo Loop, about 15 kilometres from Mopani Rest Camp. Trail guests meet the guides at lunchtime in Mopani Camp; to get there on time, they should allow three hours from the nearest gate at Phalaborwa, with viewing stops included. The camping area at Fraser's Rest is shaded by trees and is next to a waterhole, so close-up wildlife encounters can be expected.

Unlike Sand River Bush Camp, Nyarhi is designed for campers who are totally self-sufficient. As well as rooftop-tents, trailer tents, or off-road caravans, gear should include bedding, a camping fridge, a gas stove, a shower bag, cooking utensils, camp chairs, a table, solar lamps and head torches. As there's no water on site, guests should bring at least 50 litres of water per person for drinking, washing and cooking (guests prepare their own food). There are Enviro Loos and shower screens at the camp. The only other permanent feature of the camp is a concrete slab for the fire. Braai grids are supplied along with some firewood, but there's no harm in bringing extra wood along.

Each day two trail guides lead walks from the camp, with the timing determined by conditions and in consultation with the group. The walks are not too arduous and cover a distance of five to ten kilometres, with the emphasis being on enjoying time in the bush. The terrain is gentle, a mix of mopane woodlands and riverine trees. On the fourth day guests depart from the camp before 10:00.

A natural spring near Nyarhi camp is the place to enjoy sundowners (left) and to watch elephant bulls engage in mock battle (right).

Kruger Trail

The ultimate wild walk in South Africa is the Kruger Trail, which traverses the entire park from Crooks Corner in the north-east to Malelane in the south. The distance covered totals 600–650 kilometres, with participants hiking six legs of about 100 kilometres each at intervals over three years.

The trail is organised and led by the SHR corps as part of their fundraising role. The idea originated with members from the Magalies Region (Tshwane/ Pretoria), and was first offered in 2018. The trail is designed for groups rather than individuals, and places are strictly limited; they can only be booked via an annual auction. This is held each October for walks starting the following year on specific dates from May to September, and once a group wins a starting date, future legs of the trail are charged at a fixed rate.

Hikers are accompanied by Honorary Rangers and must be totally self-sufficient, as the walks are unsupported. As the trail traverses extremely wild areas, with unknown water sources, it is best suited for experienced bush walkers capable of carrying heavy loads in hot conditions. Each leg must be undertaken in sequence, and comprises six days of walking and five nights camping in the bushveld. The closest SANParks rest camp is used as a base before and after each leg. Hikers use their own vehicles to access the trailheads, with the lead guide's coordination. After a night at Punda Maria Rest Camp, the first stage is hiked from Crooks Corner to Vlakteplaas, with subsequent stages ending in Mopani Rest Camp, Olifants Rest Camp, N'wanetsi Picnic Spot, Lower Sabie Rest Camp and finally through the scenic Thlalabye hills to complete the epic journey at a cairn close to the Malelane Satellite Camp.

■ Walk type	Backpacking trail
■ Booking	www.thekrugertrail.com
■ Cost category	Under R1,500
■ Group size	6–8
■ Min. age	16
■ Season	May–September

The need to carry supplies for five nights makes the Kruger Trail the most demanding walking safari in South Africa.

SANParks Honorary Rangers

RHINO WALKING SAFARIS

■ Walk type	Wilderness trail
■ Booking	www.rws.co.za
■ Cost category	R3,000–R6,000
■ Group size	2–8
■ Min. age	12
■ Season	January–December

Guests make their way to the treehouse in the Rhino Walking concession area.

To the north of Skukuza Rest Camp in the Kruger National Park is a 12,000-hectare private concession managed by Seolo Africa. The concession provides one of the highest-rated walking safari experiences in South Africa. It shares 15 kilometres of unfenced boundary with Sabi Sands Game Reserve, a private reserve to the west, and the wildlife density is high.

The main base of the concession is Rhino Post Safari Lodge, where guests can take part in game drives. Walking safaris are run by Rhino Walking Safaris and operate from Plains Camp, about 30 minutes by game-viewing vehicle from Rhino Post. Here, four luxury tents are nestled under a thicket of knob thorn trees. This is camping in style, and each tent is crafted of canvas and wood with an en-suite bathroom and hot water.

A highlight for the adventurous is the chance to spend a night at a treehouse Sleep-Out deck. These four platforms are five to eight kilometres away from Plains Camp, depending on the route walked, and overlook the Xiteveteve Waterhole. Dinner is eaten al fresco, cooked in traditional braai style over an open fire. Then guests climb about four metres above ground to sleep in safety as animals roam the unfenced camp below. After a day on foot in the bush, nothing but a mosquito net and some canvas separates sleepers from the nocturnal sounds of Africa.

Walking safaris operate from either the camp or the Sleep-Out location, but not from both at once. So, when a Sleep-Out is booked, all subsequent guest bookings for those nights will be there also.

Two well-qualified guides lead groups on morning and afternoon walks; they have a wealth of experience of all things natural and enjoy sharing it. The walks typically last for two to three hours, but can extend up to five hours depending on sightings, conditions and guests' wishes. The terrain is mainly flat with thorn bushveld and marula woodlands, and every walk is a different exploration. As well as looking out for interesting plants, insects and birds, hikers may also encounter all the big game, from buffalo and elephant to big cats and African wild dogs.

The treehouse decks near Plains Camp overlook the Xiteveteve Waterhole.

After the early walks and brunch, guests can relax on the deck overlooking the Timbetene Plain and waterhole. In the afternoon, there's the chance of a game drive, which can incorporate a shorter walk if everyone is up for it.

The Plains Camp is operated on an all-inclusive basis, so tariffs cover accommodation, meals, most drinks and walking safaris, and there's a minimum two-night stay. Be sure to request the Sleep-Out at the time of booking, if you want to experience this option.

SINGITA SWENI LODGE

Singita Sweni Lodge is one of 10 luxury private lodges in the Kruger National Park, and one of two lodges operated by Singita within the park. Other properties in the Singita family can be found in Sabi Sands to the west of the Kruger Park, as well as in Zimbabwe, Tanzania and Rwanda.

Located not far from SANParks's Sweni Wilderness Trail camp, east of Satara Rest Camp, the lodge is set in a 33,000-hectare private concession and offers an extremely luxurious experience. As at the other Singita lodges in South Africa, all guides are qualified to lead trails, which means that guests are not confined to the vehicle on game drives and can get down to enjoy a special view or feature.

Walk type	Day walk
Booking	www.singita.com
Cost category	Over R6,000
Group size	2–8
Min. age	16
Season	January–December

Walks can be arranged as the main activity of the day at the guests' request. Along with a trail guide, a tracker accompanies the group to share knowledge and help to find wildlife. The maximum group size on a walk is generally six, although up to eight people can be accommodated on request, with the addition of a second guide.

The Lebombo euphorbia is endemic to the Lebombo Mountains near Singita Sweni Lodge.

Singita Sweni Lodge is located on a hill overlooking the Sweni River, close to the confluence with the N'wanetsi River, which flows into neighbouring Mozambique a few kilometres downstream. A nearby dam on the N'wanetsi, within view of the lodge decks, ensures year-round water to attract wildlife. The varied terrain of savannah, gorges and rocky ridges makes for a diverse range of walking options.

Although walks may start from the lodge, it's usual to travel by game-viewing vehicle to explore a particular habitat. Guides decide on the routes in consultation with guests, taking into account the walk duration, weather conditions and animal movements. Some walks explore the N'wanetsi and Xinkelengane rivers and their riparian woodlands, which include sycamore figs, fever trees, leadwood and jackalberry trees. One expedition starts at the Granophyre Ridge, meandering past dramatic rock features to a viewpoint overlooking the N'wanetsi. From there it's possible to descend to the river and return a different way. Other areas to explore include the Lebombo Mountains, the Gudzane Dam and the Central Depression area.

JOCK SAFARI LODGE

In the heart of the southern Kruger National Park, Jock Safari Lodge is a famous and long-established luxury private concession. It is owned by the non-profit Caleo Foundation, proprietor of Sanbona Wildlife Reserve in the Western Cape. That reserve is more oriented towards wilderness walks (see chapter 14).

At Jock's, guests are offered walks year-round; these excursions are short, usually one hour. The schedule sees guests return from the morning game drive for breakfast, and then walk directly from the camp into the surrounding bushveld accompanied by two armed guides. The area has a dense wildlife population that includes leopard, elephant, rhino and buffalo.

Walk type	Day walk
Booking	www.jocksafarilodge.com
Cost category	Over R6,000
Group size	1–6
Min. age	12
Season	January–December

Guests get close to buffalo on a dawn walk at Jock Safari Lodge.

Each room at the lodge has a private deck with day beds and a plunge pool.

Lanner Gorge is a must-see in northern Kruger's Pafuri area.

RETURNAfrica

RETURNAFRICA WALK EXPERIENCES

Vast areas of sun-crisp mopane savannah are characteristic of the northern Kruger National Park. That's until you reach the river valleys of the Luvuvhu and Limpopo rivers; here fever trees, baobabs and figs proliferate, and large numbers of animals come in search of winter water. The area is commonly known as the Pafuri Triangle, named after Venda chief Maphaphuli, and is best accessed via Pafuri Gate, a seven-hour drive from Johannesburg.

According to SANParks, as much as 75 per cent of the total biodiversity of the Kruger Park occurs here, in an area only a little more than 1 per cent of its total size. Pafuri's wetlands are listed under the Ramsar Convention on Wetlands because of their international importance for birdlife. In all, it's one of the best places in Africa for a walking safari.

Lanner Gorge is at its best in the afternoon light.

RETURNAfrica

In the 1990s the area was the subject of the first successful land claim by traditional owners, the Makuleke people, who had been forcibly removed in 1969. Shangaan-speakers, their lands stretch from the upper reaches of the Luvuvhu River to the Mozambique border. By agreement, the returned land was incorporated into the Kruger Park as the 26,500-hectare Makuleke Contractual Park for a 50-year period. Today it is a prime example of how habitat and wildlife conservation can bring benefits to local communities, with the Makuleke being part-owners of the tourism facilities and receiving a share of the revenue.

There are just a few concessions in this remote corner of the park. Near the Limpopo River, the bush education company EcoTraining has a camp (see opposite page), and in the west of the Pafuri Triangle The Outpost and Pel's Post are luxury lodges that can provide walks on request. The top option is RETURNAfrica, a trails specialist, which has a selection of properties along the Luvuvhu River.

ECOTRAINING

It's rare not to learn something new on a bush walk in a South African reserve, and it's possible to formalise the education by taking a field course with a training company. The core business of these companies is to mentor and train aspiring professional guides, but they also offer courses for people interested in developing their knowledge as part of a bushveld walking holiday.

One such company is EcoTraining, which has a camp in the Makuleke Contractual Park close to the Zimbabwe border in the northern section of the Kruger National Park, with activities taking place in an area closed to park visitors. In addition to being used to train professional trail guides, the camp is the base for a number of shorter programmes that are ideal for nature enthusiasts who want to improve their knowledge while immersed in a bush trail experience.

The EcoQuest course – which can be one or two weeks long – spans the natural world from plants and animals to ecology and astronomy. The six-day Wilderness Trails Skills course covers essentials for surviving on foot in the wild, such as navigation, water-sourcing and campsite selection. Other courses focus on tracking, birding and photography. A typical day sees participants out in the early morning, returning for breakfast and lectures. After some downtime and a late lunch, there will be an afternoon outing related to the theme of the day.

The unfenced camp is located in a grove of nyala trees on the edge of the floodplain of the Limpopo River, and can accommodate 16 guests in en-suite A-frame huts. The company also runs courses in Selati and Karongwe game reserves in Limpopo, and Mashatu Game Reserve in Botswana (see chapter 20). For more information, see www.ecotraining.co.za or call +27 (0) 73 508 6019.

The fever trees and sodic pans are distinct features of the landscape in Makuleke Contractual Park.

Pafuri Camp

▦ Walk type	Day walk
▦ Booking	www.returnafrica.com
▦ Cost category	R3,000–R6,000
▦ Group size	2–8
▦ Min. age	16
▦ Season	January–December

RETURNAfrica's permanent Pafuri Camp is located directly beside the Luvuvhu River, with well-appointed en-suite tents shaded by riparian woodland. The accommodation units, pool and dining area overlook the water, perfect for wildlife watching, and the camp is unfenced, so spontaneous close animal encounters are not unusual.

Habitats in the Makuleke Contractual Park range from deep sandstone gorges on the western boundary to sodic pans and fever tree forest in the floodplains, to the confluence of the Limpopo and Luvuvhu rivers on the eastern boundary. The stand-out walks explore the fever tree forest and Lanner Gorge. The first is really special, a large mature forest of elegant fever trees on a floodplain. Habitat like this is rare in the Kruger Park, as trees are under constant attack by everything from insects to elephants. Somehow the scale and speedy growth of the trees here has led to a magical expanse where the walking is level and shady. Lanner Gorge, by contrast, is an ancient U-shaped valley carved over millennia by the Luvuvhu River. It takes over an hour to drive to the trailhead for the Lanner, but it's worth it. Another popular option takes walkers to the confluence point of the Luvuvhu and Limpopo rivers at Crook's Corner, from where Zimbabwe and Mozambique can be seen across the river.

RETURNAfrica

All guest tents and common areas at Pafuri Camp overlook the wildlife-rich Luvuvhu River.

RETURNAfrica

The rustic and blissfully low-key Hutwini Trails Camp is used for ReturnAfrica's walking safaris.

The usual format of walks from the main camp is to set out by game-viewing vehicle at dawn, which gives walkers an opportunity to spot wildlife en route to a place of interest. Once the destination is reached, the group leaves the vehicle to explore on foot, led by two guides. The length of the walk is tuned to guests' wishes. After returning to camp for breakfast, guests can relax and view wildlife from the poolside or dining area. Another drive takes place in the late afternoon, ending with sundowners at a suitable point.

In addition to the main camp, the nearby Baobab Hill Bush House is an exclusive homestead available for group bookings. Formerly the area ranger's house, it can accommodate up to eight guests.

RETURNAfrica tariffs include full board, drives and walks. To make the most of travel time, some visitors fly in to the private airstrip close by. There is a conservation levy payable per person per booking, which is in addition to the SANParks daily conservation fee and not covered by the Wild Card.

Pafuri Walking Safaris

For a really immersive experience, between April and October, walkers can stay at the only seasonal wilderness trail camp in the Kruger National Park. At the start of each walking season Hutwini Trails Camp is set up, and then entirely removed when summer arrives.

Guests may choose to spend a night or two at the main Pafuri Camp before transferring to the Hutwini Camp, which is set under ana trees a few steps from the Luvuvhu River. On

■ Walk type	Wilderness trail
■ Booking	www.returnafrica.com
■ Cost category	R1,500–R3,000
■ Group size	2–8
■ Min. age	16
■ Season	April–October

Trail guide Alweet Hlungwani shares his knowledge of termite nests and the role these insects play in the ecosystem.

Animals have right of passage through the camp.

The middle of the day is relaxation time for guests.

the first day, guests receive a gentle introduction to the terrain with an afternoon walk from the camp. On the following days, they can expect a very early call for the main walk of the day. It's usual to drive to the starting point in order to explore different areas each day. Walks last three to four hours, and cover anything from four to ten kilometres, depending on the conditions and what animals the group encounters. Back at the camp after the walk, guests are welcomed with chilled towels before brunch is served. Then there is time to relax and observe the wildlife that frequents the unfenced camp and nearby river. With their batteries recharged, guests go on another outing in the afternoon. This can be a walk or a drive, depending on guests' wishes and what wildlife is encountered.

There's a minimum two-night stay for this trail, which makes sense given the distance to this remote corner of the park. A typical visit to the fly camp would be for three nights, which is ideal for unwinding and experiencing the different habitats in the area, but longer stays are not hard to justify.

RETURNAfrica also offers special trails at certain times of the year. The Luvuvhu Discovery Trail is a seven-night adventure which is partly slackpacking – wild camping with walkers' gear transferred by vehicle. It's offered on a selection of dates from April to October. Of the seven nights, one is spent at the Baobab Hill Bush Lodge, three on the trail, sleeping out under the stars, and three at the Hutwini Trail Camp. If slackpacking sounds too soft, backpacking is also a possibility, and guests can disappear into the bush for a few days carrying everything they need for survival.

It's worth checking the RETURNAfrica website for other enticing specials, such as trails led by Ju/'hoansi San (Bushman) trackers, renowned as the most skilled in Africa.

The Pafuri region in the northern sector of the Kruger National Park is of international importance for birdlife and is home to the Makuleke Wetlands, a designated Ramsar Wetlands site. More than 277 species of bird can be found here, with a small selection shown below.

Paul Rigsby

Pel's fishing owl

RETURNAfrica

Saddle-billed storks

RETURNAfrica

Southern red-billed hornbill

RETURNAfrica

Black-throated wattle-eye

RETURNAfrica

Amur falcon

Cooling my feet in Pafuri

Honestly, we spent the whole morning hiking barefoot in the Kruger. Our toes sank into soft sand as we entered the Luvuvhu River and began wading calf-deep into a shady gorge. It's surely the park's most beautiful river, clear and ever-flowing, and for our guide, Calvin de la Rey, it's one of his favourite places to take guests. The wildlife loves it too, and the area teems with animals and birdlife. A couple of times we moved to the banks to skirt deeper pools, stepping carefully through thorny hot sands. We didn't need to be reminded of how big the crocodiles are in these parts. Let me tell.

The Hutwini Trails Camp, operated in the cooler months by Pafuri Walking Safaris, is on the bank of the Luvuvhu in the shade of Natal mahogany and ana trees. Nyala are more or less permanent residents, and the day before we arrived, one had expired in the camp. For obvious reasons, it had been removed to the riverbed for nature to deal with the carcass. On the first day, nothing touched it. On the second day, we returned from a long walk to find about 40 vultures, lappet-faced and white-backed, getting down to business. And on the third day, there was no trace of the nyala. We examined the sands and found the perfect indentations of a crocodile. Calvin paced it to measure four metres. The marks showed how it had shifted position with each powerful haul on the heavy carcass.

Denis Costello

Clear and sandy, the Luvuvhu River is suited to barefoot exploration.

The unfenced camp is immersed in nature, and feels part of the forest, not a place apart. Gladys, our cook, cheerfully told us we'd missed seeing a leopard that had strolled by her kitchen. We also had a visit from an elephant, which stepped gently around the camp furniture, pruning trees.

Apart from the beauty of the area, the best thing about walks in the Pafuri area is the diversity of the terrain, and the flexibility to decide where to go each day.

A walk in the fever tree forest is a must.

The longest walk took us from the stunning fever tree forest back to camp via a series of shallow pans. The fever trees are a real favourite, a picture-perfect yellow-green forest that seeded in a flood about half a century ago. The tree's name comes from the time of European explorers, who contracted malaria while camping in their shade, and blamed the trees. As we walked, the air filled with the scent of wild sage.

While we picnicked overlooking a pan, we kept still as a series of drinkers arrived: a pair of black-backed jackals, a herd of impala, and zebra close behind. All of these animals find it hard to discern people unless they move – unlike the baboons, whose eyes work like ours. They spotted us from 300 metres away and raised a fuss which startled the drinkers.

On our last day we relaxed by walking to the nearby Hutwini Gorge, for which the trail camp is named. This break in the ridge is a natural highway for animals going to water, and a perfect ambush site for predators. Calvin told us how he watches elephants move nervously through it, almost as if they recall the days of human traps. Ironically, after our barefoot venture, it was here that Calvin got a bite from an ant that took advantage of a hole in his velskoens. **HM**

Black-backed jackal came to drink at the pan.

Camping wild in the Kruger National Park is an unforgettable experience.

AFRICAN-BORN SAFARIS

From its headquarters in Cape Town, African-Born Safaris organises bespoke itineraries throughout southern and East Africa. Its founders are experienced trail guides who love getting into the wilds on foot, so it's not surprising that walking safaris are a core element of their business. In South Africa, the company offers walks in a number of reserves, including the Makuleke Contractual Park in the far north of the Kruger National Park. There, in partnership with RETURNAfrica, African-Born Safaris runs the Walk Pafuri experience, with guests staying at the comfortable Hutwini Trails Camp (see page 115). The camp serves as a base from which daily guided walks are undertaken to explore the diverse ecology of the area – from Lanner Gorge in the west to Crooks Corner in the east. In the evenings, the well-travelled guides share their trove of bush lore and adventures with guests at the camp.

To meet the increasing demand for more authentic bushveld immersions, the company began leading backpacking trails in the same area. The Primitive Pafuri trails are perfect for anyone seeking a genuine wilderness experience, one shared with Africa's earliest humans. Best of all, they include an element unique in the Kruger National Park: the chance to sleep out under the stars.

Primitive Pafuri

Primitive Pafuri is the only walking safari in the Kruger National Park where hikers sleep tentless out in the wild. And what's more, it takes place in the park's most biodiverse zone, the Pafuri Triangle, in the heart of the Great Limpopo Transfrontier Conservation Area (see pages 122–123). Sleeping here in the open, surrounded by the nocturnal sounds of Africa, with just a small fire for company, guarantees a special wilderness experience.

■ Walk type	Backpacking trail
■ Booking	www.africanbornsafaris.com
■ Cost category	R1,500-R3,000
■ Group size	6–8
■ Min. age	16
■ Season	April–October

The terrain in the eastern sector of the Pafuri Triangle is mostly flat, and is dominated by the floodplains of the Limpopo and Luvuvhu rivers, seasonal pans and magnificent

fever tree forests. To the west, the Luvuvhu River enters the Kruger Park through a dramatic gorge, and walks here can include scrambles on steeper slopes, studded with baobabs.

Hikers on a Primitive Pafuri trail venture into the veld carrying everything they need to survive for three or four nights, and they have to be fit enough to carry a backpack weighing up to 15 kilograms. Guests have to supply their own kit and food, and the company provides a packing list in advance. They are also willing to source items for you, an especially useful service for overseas travellers.

A guide scans the veld from one of the many vantage points in Pafuri.

In order to safely manage the night watch rota, the minimum group size is six, accompanied by two guides. On a typical day, the main walking is done early to take advantage of cooler temperatures, with the distance ranging between six and twelve kilometres. A suitable camp location, close to a water source and safe from animal traffic, is found at the end of each day's walk. Water is obtained from the Luvuvhu River or scooped from holes dug in the sand, naturally filtered to potable quality.

Each Primitive Pafuri trail is tailored to suit the wishes and capacities of the guests, the aim being an enjoyable experience rather than an endurance challenge. The trails are ideal for groups of family or friends, but singles and couples can join pre-booked groups, subject to the limit on the maximum number of people per party.

There is covered parking for self-drive guests at the main RETURNAfrica camp, a 30-minute drive from Pafuri Gate and 1.5 hours from Punda Maria Gate. African-Born Safaris can also organise shuttles from OR Tambo International Airport in Johannesburg and other locations, or guests can fly into Pafuri Airstrip in the Makuleke Contractual Park. It's nice to include a night or two after the trail in the RETURNAfrica camp, to soak up its comforts before the onward journey.

If there are four or fewer participants on a Primitive Pafuri trail, night watch is cancelled, making it necessary for walkers to sleep in tents so that everyone gets enough sleep.

THE 'RUSSIAN DOLLS OF LIMPOPO'

At two million hectares, the Kruger National Park is big, but not big enough. The natural migration routes of herding grazers such as elephant, buffalo, zebra and wildebeest are constrained by man-made boundaries, with negative outcomes that include overgrazing, tree destruction, famine and culling. It is well understood that the solution to this problem is to remove barriers and expand the territory in which wildlife can roam, while also ensuring that the many communities that live and work in the surrounding area are involved in decision making and benefit from conservation strategies.

Klaserie Sands

The Greater Kruger features a host of walking opportunities from backpacking to ultra-luxury.

Working with these communities, conservationists are busy creating an enormous area of contiguous protected habitat. An extension to the Kruger Park can be found along the Limpopo River in the far north of the park: the Makuleke Contractual Park is a community-owned, legally separate entity (see page 112) that is managed under contract by SANParks as part of the Kruger. It is usually represented as part of the park on maps. Thereafter, like a set of Russian dolls, the national park is nested in a series of protected lands.

ACROSS THE BORDERS

The first 'doll' enclosing the Kruger is the Great Limpopo Transfrontier Park (GLTP), a contiguous area which comprises the Kruger National Park, Limpopo National Park in Mozambique, Zimbabwe's Gonarezhou National Park, and the Sengwe Corridor communal land that connects Gonarezhou and the Kruger Park. Progress in developing the GLTP is slow, and 20 years after its establishment much of the Kruger Park's eastern boundary fence with Mozambique is still standing. Visitors can drive across the international border from the Kruger Park into Limpopo National Park, but attempts to establish walking safaris on the Mozambique side have been unsuccessful.

THE FENCELESS WEST

The South African reserves on the western boundary of the Kruger Park are marketed as 'Greater Kruger'. About 180,000 hectares of high-quality wilderness is conserved here, most of which shares a boundary with the publicly owned national park. Greater Kruger lands are in a mix of private, provincial and community ownership, with the fences between them removed in 1993–94, allowing a natural east–west migration that has enabled both wildlife and tourism to flourish.

The Greater Kruger reserves offer wonderful opportunities for walking safaris and contain dozens of lodges and camps, many of which have qualified trail guides. The area includes Sabi Sands and Mala Mala north of the Sabie River, and the Manyeleti Private Nature Reserve (see chapter 6) north of Sabi Sands. Further north again, a group of reserves in the upper reaches of the Olifants and Timbavati rivers cooperate as the Associated Private Nature Reserves (APNR) (see chapters 6, 7 and 8). Beyond the town of Phalaborwa are the Makuya and Letaba Ranch (see chapter 9) reserves. The extent of the Greater Kruger was formalised in 2020 in the SANParks-led Greater Kruger Strategic Development Plan.

THE TEN MILLION-HECTARE DREAM

The fourth and biggest 'doll' is an even larger conservation project known as the Great Limpopo Transfrontier Conservation Area (GLTFCA), which spans almost ten million hectares. In addition to the Great Limpopo Transfrontier Park, it includes the Greater Kruger reserves, vast areas of recovering wilderness in Mozambique, and various private and state-owned conservation areas in South Africa and Zimbabwe adjacent to the transfrontier park.

South Africa is a partner in six transfrontier parks, and there are a number of others in Africa. The driving force behind them is the Peace Parks Foundation, established in 1997 by HRH Prince Bernhard of the Netherlands, President Nelson Mandela and Dr Anton Rupert. For more information about the GLTP and GLTFCA, see www.peaceparks.org.

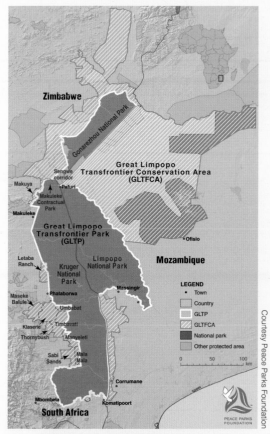

A dream in the making: the Great Limpopo Transfrontier Conservation Area will conserve almost ten million hectares of wilderness.

Courtesy Peace Parks Foundation

6 ▪ MANYELETI PRIVATE NATURE RESERVE

Russell Hine

Manyeleti's main dam has a healthy population of resident hippo.

Manyeleti Private Nature Reserve is a well-positioned reserve sharing a long, open boundary with the Kruger National Park to the east and Sabi Sands Game Reserve to the south. The 23,000-hectare reserve – the name Manyeleti means 'place of stars' – also has an unfenced boundary with the Timbavati Private Nature Reserve to the north. It differs from Timbavati and the other Associated Private Nature Reserves in that it is owned by the local Mnisi Shangaan community, who gain an income from the concession fees paid by the lodges and camps, and also benefit from employment there.

During the apartheid years, Manyeleti was the only reserve in the area that was open to non-white visitors. Today, it is a quiet destination, with just a handful of private concessions. Although there are no perennial rivers, the watercourses are well wooded, and the reserve's geographic situation results in good numbers of game animals in residence and traversing the area. The extensive palatable grasslands attract herds of buffalo over 300 strong. These and other grazers provide good feeding for predators, and there are at least two large resident lion prides, while other prides move between Manyeleti, Sabi Sands and the Kruger Park.

Pungwe Safari Camp is an intimate camp, offering comfort with a touch of rustic charm.

WALKING IN MANYELETI PRIVATE NATURE RESERVE

Manyeleti shares the same lowveld climate as the southern part of the Kruger Park – warm to hot throughout the year, with rainfall confined for the most part to the summer months. It's possible to walk all year round, although it is better to avoid the months from November to February. In March and April the bushveld can be a bit dense, but from May onwards walking conditions improve. The nights in June and July can be chilly.

The ridges above the seep line have coarse granitic soils that result in a lower grass density, and so make for excellent walking amidst open broadleaved woodlands dominated by marula trees and bushwillow. There is one specialist walking operator in Manyeleti, Pungwe Safari Camp.

PUNGWE SAFARI CAMP

Pungwe Safari Camp offers dawn walks of three to four hours throughout the year, with a game drive in the afternoon. The unfenced camp has limited solar power and water from a borehole, and the en-suite tents offer hot showers via a traditional donkey boiler over an open fire.

The 10,000-hectare walking area is in the southern part of the reserve bordering the Kruger Park and Sabi Sands, and has few game drive roads. During a stay at Pungwe, it's rare to see another vehicle or human, apart from the small group at the trail camp. Walkers will probably encounter buffalo, zebra and wildebeest, and browsers such as kudu and giraffe, as well as enjoying the many smaller treasures of flora and fauna.

Walk type	Day walk
Booking	www.pungwe.co.za
Cost category	R3,000–R6,000
Group size	1–8
Min. age	14
Season	January–December

7 ■ TIMBAVATI PRIVATE NATURE RESERVE

Lowveld Trails Company

The Nhlaralumi River flows only a couple of times each year; when it is dry, walkers stay close to the verdant river banks where the trees provide much-needed shade.

Like Manyeleti, Timbavati Private Nature Reserve has a long and unfenced eastern boundary with the Kruger National Park from Orpen Gate northwards. It's about seven hours by road from Johannesburg. It is a member of the Associated Private Nature Reserves group, and as it has open boundaries with other large reserves to the west and north, healthy populations of the full range of big game can be found there. The widest unfenced east–west animal migration route in the lowveld stretches almost 100 kilometres from the western boundary of the Klaserie Private Nature Reserve (see chapter 8) to the Kruger Park's Mozambique frontier, and Timbavati spans 53,000 hectares in the middle of it. Several tributaries of the Olifants River, the largest being the Nhlaralumi, traverse the reserve from south to north through typical lowveld bushveld habitat. Although they only flow occasionally after summer rain, the drainage line waterholes are a major water source for wildlife.

WALKING IN TIMBAVATI PRIVATE NATURE RESERVE

The best walking season in Timbavati is April to September, after the summer heat has abated. The ideal months are April, May, August and September, which offer pleasant day temperatures in the mid-20s Celsius while avoiding the colder nights of midwinter.

Several lodges in Timbavati run dawn walks, including Bateleur Safari Camp and Ngala Safari Lodge. For multi-day trails there are three stand-out options: Lowveld Trails Company, Tanda Tula Field Camp and Simbavati Trails Camp. The two luxury field camps don't operate in summer, but Lowveld Trails Company leads backpacking trails year-round.

BATELEUR SAFARI CAMP

Attractively located in dense woodland at a bend in the Nhlaralumi River, Bateleur Safari Camp comprises eight comfortable canvas-walled, en-suite units overlooking the sandy riverbed. The camp has a basic electric 'elephant fence', so smaller wildlife wanders through at will while elephant, buffalo and rhino can be spotted visiting the seasonal waterhole.

Of the many private lodges in the Greater Kruger region, Bateleur is one of the few that has a strong focus on walking safaris, and it has several highly qualified trail guides and trackers in residence. The lodge has a 10,000-hectare walking zone, so there is plenty of variety available. The format is flexible to accommodate guests' wishes – from a short stroll as part of a game drive to longer three- to four-hour dawn walks in place of a drive. Walks may start from the camp, or use a game-viewing vehicle to access another zone. There are enough guides to allow for situations where some guests opt for a dawn game drive while others choose a walk at the same time.

Senior tracker Temba Brown explains the dentition of buffalo.

Walk type	Day walk
Booking	www.bateleursafaricamp.com
Cost category	R3,000–R6,000
Group size	1–8
Min. age	12
Season	January–December

A riparian woodland shelters Bateleur Safari Camp.

Back at camp, the guides are happy to teach guests some bush survival skills such as lighting fires and making ropes and water containers from bush materials. This is fun and interesting, and not usually offered by lodges.

On certain dates in the cooler part of the year the lodge offers the unique On Track @ Bateleur Experience. This involves learning tracking skills from experts, and includes practical experience in finding animals and following their tracks. It's a good option for corporate bookings, as up to 16 guests can be accommodated. Individuals may also be included, but the minimum booking number for the On Track programme is six, and the minimum stay is three nights.

TANDA TULA FIELD CAMP

Tanda Tula Field Camp is a sister to the Tanda Tula Safari Camp in the Timbavati reserve, which has a large exclusive game-viewing area bordering the Kruger National Park. The luxurious field camp is established for each private group that books it, with all traces removed afterwards.

Designed for walking safaris, the camp is offered in the drier months from the start of March to the end of September and has a minimum stay requirement of three nights. It's one of the more expensive walking safaris in South Africa but guests can expect every comfort, fine cuisine and excellent guides. The daily plan is tailored to guests' wishes and special interests.

The camp is set in the central eastern part of Timbavati, where a series of drainage lines run northwards to join the Olifants River. Although usually dry, they support extensive riparian woodlands that are a pleasure to explore. For variety, walks also meander into the watershed bushveld where elephant, buffalo and rhino feed. The centre of Timbavati is well situated for migrating game such as zebra and wildebeest, which move west in summer in search of grazing. It is also prime lion territory, and African wild dogs and cheetah are sometimes spotted.

After dark, the air is filled with the sounds of nocturnal creatures.

After the morning walk, guests return to a hot shower and brunch. The middle of the day is spent relaxing at camp, spotting birds and camp visitors. Wildlife moves freely through the unfenced camp, making it important to follow the guidance of staff when moving around, especially after dark. Afternoon tea is followed by a shorter walk, sundowners in the veld, and a short game drive which provides a chance to look for evening prowlers such as hyena, porcupine and leopard.

■ Walk type	Wilderness trail
■ Booking	www.tandatula.com
■ Cost category	Over R6,000
■ Group size	4–8
■ Min. age	14
■ Season	March–September

SIMBAVATI TRAILS CAMP

The Simbavati collection of safari lodges and camps is located in the remote northern extreme of Timbavati Reserve. Between this corner of the reserve and the Timbavati River to the east is a 15,000-hectare portion of land that forms part of the Kruger National Park. This land is zoned as wilderness, denoting its pristine status (see the box on Kruger National Park zoning on page 93). There are no fences between the two conservation areas to obstruct the movement of wildlife, making this excellent walking territory.

A recent addition to the family is the Simbavati Trails Camp, dedicated to walking safaris. The comfortable camp is established for the duration of the walking season alongside an ephemeral river. There are four tents, each with an en-suite flush toilet and a bucket shower that is filled with warm water when required. Apart from these comforts, the camp is off-grid – no power, no phone signal, no Wi-Fi, just the chance to unwind in a remote corner of the lowveld. Solar chargers are provided for small devices.

Each day, an experienced trail guide leads dawn walks, which are about three hours long. The walks, conducted at a gentle pace, explore the seasonal drainage lines in mixed bushveld on mostly level terrain. There are a couple of dams in the walking zone, with hippos in residence. Trail snacks and water are provided for rest breaks.

Simbavati's fly camp (top and above) is set up at the start of each operating season.

■ Walk type	Wilderness trail
■ Booking	www.simbavati.com
■ Cost category	R3,000–R6,000
■ Group size	1–8
■ Min. age	16
■ Season	March–November

The group returns to camp by midmorning, where brunch is served in the dining tent. The middle part of the day is devoted to relaxation, and there's a deck with loungers and a small plunge pool for cooling down. As temperatures drop, there's another walk in the afternoon, with the aim of ending up at a scenic spot for a rendezvous with the game-viewing vehicle and sundowners.

Meals are prepared by the camp cook over an open fire, and served either in the dining tent or outdoors in the boma. In this remote zone there is little light pollution, so it's a good spot for stargazing.

It's recommended that guests stay for three nights, so that two days can be devoted to walks. Guests over the age of 65 should bring a doctor's certificate of fitness with them. It's not possible to self-drive to the Simbavati lodges, and arrangements for transfers will be made upon booking.

LOWVELD TRAILS COMPANY WALK EXPERIENCES

The Lowveld Trails Company leads bush walks in Timbavati for the adventurous and very adventurous, with one option offering the rare opportunity to experience sleeping under the stars in a big game area.

The company is operated by two of the country's most highly regarded trail guides. As well as running trails, it provides training for aspiring field guides and mentorship for those building their number of bushveld hours and encounters. The company can provide options for transfers, or directions for parking and a pick-up service for self-drivers. Bookings are offered on a group basis (with the same price for any group size up to eight) and trails take a break between mid-December and mid-January.

There are two main trail variations, both offering three nights in the bush: the Tented Camp Experience and the Primitive Trail.

Digging in a riverbed to source clean water is part of the wild camping experience.

Tented Camp Experience

Walkers taking the Tented Camp Experience are based in a fly camp that is set up and removed for each trail, minimising the eco-logical impact. The two-person dome tents are pitched alongside a dry riverbed in the

■ Walk type	Wilderness trail
■ Booking	www.lowveldtrails.co.za
■ Cost category	R1,500–R3,000
■ Group size	1–8
■ Min. age	12
■ Season	January–December

Hikers on the Primitive Trail take turns to keep night watch by a small fire.

shade of jackalberry trees, and there's no fencing. Ablutions are simple, with pit latrines and bucket showers with canvas screening.

Mattresses and pillows are supplied, but participants should bring their own sleeping bags. Guests can self-cater, or opt for a fully catered trail option, with cooking taking place on gas stoves and the campfire. Water is supplied at the camp, and cooler boxes and ice are provided for drinks (guests should bring their own). For self-caterers, a solar-powered fridge is available.

A game-viewing vehicle is used to travel to the camp from the meeting point at the Bush Pub & Inn outside the Timbavati reserve gate, and is available to provide flexibility on where to walk each day.

Walks depart at first light after a snack of rusks and coffee, and walkers just need to carry the essentials in a day pack. Each day a different area is explored for four to five hours, with the group returning around midday for brunch. There follow a few hours to relax before a light lunch at 15:00, and an afternoon walk of two to three hours. Dinner is taken by the campfire, and camp chairs are provided.

Primitive Trail

The Lowveld Trails Company's Primitive Trail is a step up in wildness. This is a sleep-out trail, similar to the Primitive Pafuri experience in the Pafuri Triangle (see page 120) – hikers sleep under the stars, taking turns to keep watch by a small fire, alone with their thoughts. Each night is spent in a different place, with no fixed routes, and hikers need to carry the essentials for three nights in the wild.

Walk type	Backpacking trail
Booking	www.lowveldtrails.co.za
Cost category	Under R1,500
Group size	1–8
Min. age	16
Season	January–December

For as long as the water table level allows, water for washing and drinking is sourced from holes dug in the riverbed. Filtered through the sand, it's usually clean and does not require treatment. It's hard to imagine a more authentic way to become immersed in the African wilderness.

8 ■ KLASERIE PRIVATE NATURE RESERVE

Klaserie Sands

The landscape at Klaserie Private Nature Reserve turns verdant and lush after the summer rains.

To the north-west of Timbavati Private Nature Reserve is Klaserie Private Nature Reserve which, at 60,000 hectares, is the largest of the Associated Private Nature Reserves. It was proclaimed a nature reserve in 1972, after local farmers agreed to combine their farmlands into a single conservation area. Today the reserve has unfenced boundaries with its neigbhours: the Maseke Balule Game Reserve to the west, the Umbabat Private Nature Reserve to the east, and the Kruger National Park to the north-east.

The main geographic feature of the reserve is the Klaserie River, a tributary of the Olifants River. It is dry, except in times of prolonged rainfall in the catchment along the Mpumalanga Drakensberg escarpment.

WALKING IN KLASERIE PRIVATE NATURE RESERVE

In common with the rest of the lowveld, the preferred walking season in the Klaserie Reserve is in the drier and cooler months from April to September.

The reserve is home to several high-end lodges that provide dawn walks, including Senalala Luxury Safari Camp. What makes it ideal for walking safaris is the two specialist wilderness trail operations in the reserve, both offering year-round activities. Africa on Foot runs day walks throughout the year in Klaserie Reserve and a dry-season wilderness trail in a nearby reserve. In the north of the reserve, luxury wilderness trails are operated by Klaserie Sands Safari Trails.

AFRICA ON FOOT WALK EXPERIENCES

Part of the Sun Destinations group, Africa on Foot is a specialist and highly regarded walking safari operator. Year-round walks operate from a permanent camp on the Klaserie River, and a seasonal wilderness trail runs in the adjacent community-owned Maseke Balule Reserve.

Day walks

Africa on Foot's headquarters are near the Klaserie River, where a rustic camp has five brick chalets, two of which are family units. There's a fun treehouse option a little distance away at no extra cost. The camp has an elephant fence, but smaller animals come and go freely. In keeping with its wild credentials, the camp does not have electricity, but solar power is provided for charging devices and room lighting. Water is gas-heated. There's a camp bar with a selection of local beers, wine, soft drinks and spirits, and gas-powered refrigeration. Walking activities are included in overnight tariffs.

■ Walk type	Day walk
■ Booking	www.africaonfoot.com
■ Cost category	R3,000–R6,000
■ Group size	1–8
■ Min. age	16
■ Season	January–December

From the base camp a pair of guides take guests on two- to three-hour walks in the mornings, and game drives in the afternoons. In summer, rising time is 05:00 and in winter 05:45, with walks returning to camp by 09:00 for breakfast. The walks take place in an area with high wildlife density, and guests often encounter elephant, rhino, buffalo and giraffe. The daily combination of walks and drives provides a good variety of experiences, with the chance to get much closer to big game on the drives. As the drives continue after sunset, it's also an opportunity to spot night predators, including leopard and hyena.

Getting this close to lions on foot is a rare thrill.

Africa on Foot Wilderness Trails

For an even wilder experience, walkers should aim for the dry season from April to November. This is when the Africa on Foot Wilderness Trails operate in Maseke Balule Reserve west of Timbavati. This reserve is transected by the Olifants River and surrounded by other reserves, including the Kruger National Park to the north, so is just as rich in wildlife as the Klaserie Reserve. The wilderness trails run over three nights in slackpacking style, with each night spent in a different location. The walking area is topographically diverse and spans both sides of the upper Olifants River, making for a varied experience each day.

■ Walk type	Wilderness trail
■ Booking	www.wilderness-trails.co.za
■ Cost category	R1,500–R3,000
■ Group size	1–8
■ Min. age	16
■ Season	April–November

Guests are woken before dawn to find hot water in a camp washbasin outside their tent. Once walkers depart, the camp is taken down and transferred to the next location. The morning walk is three to four hours, with a picnic brunch taken on the trail. The aim is to reach camp by 15:00 for a snack, wash and rest. In the late afternoon there's a shorter walk or game drive, and sunset drinks.

It's a comfortable camping experience. Walkers sleep in two-person, stand-up canvas dome tents with real beds and solar lanterns; bucket showers and chemical toilets are provided. The trails are fully catered, with meals taken seated at camp tables before the day winds down around the campfire.

Em Gatland

Africa on Foot's slackpacking format facilitates comfortable pop-up camps with spacious tents.

Each of the four tents at the Klaserie Sands Safari Trails camp is secluded and shaded.

KLASERIE SANDS SAFARI TRAILS

Sheltered by trees and overlooking a dry river course in the north of the reserve, the Klaserie Sands Safari Trails camp offers an authentic wilderness immersion, albeit one with a high degree of comfort. The luxury tents have en-suite bathrooms, and each has a private timber deck overlooking the riverbed where elephants dig in the sand for water. Bushveld romantics can overnight at the Explorers' Post Sleep-Out Deck, a two-person tent on a raised platform sheltered by a weeping boer-bean tree and overlooking a hippo wallow.

■ Walk type	Wilderness trail
■ Booking	www.klaseriesands-safaritrails.com
■ Cost category	R3,000–R6,000
■ Group size	1–8
■ Min. age	16
■ Season	January–December

The camp is walking-safari focused, with a 1,000-hectare area that is for the exclusive use of Klaserie Sands Safari Trails guests. The territory extends as far as the Olifants River in the north and the unfenced boundary to the Kruger National Park in the northeast. Expert guides – who are also qualified trackers – lead three- to four-hour dawn walks that explore the mopane shrubveld and the riparian forest with its prolific birdlife.

Breakfast is taken in the wild, following a rendezvous with a game-viewing vehicle. There is a chance for close wildlife encounters during the drive back to camp, where the middle of the day is spent relaxing and enjoying a light lunch. Subject to weather conditions, a shorter walk takes place in the late afternoon, with guests enjoying sundowners at a serene location. The return drive to camp takes place in the twilight 'blue hour', offering the chance to spot emerging nocturnal animals.

Klaserie Sands Safari Trails can be booked year-round for a minimum two-night stay, and guests are always free to opt for a game drive instead of a walk.

9 ■ LETABA RANCH NATURE RESERVE

Mario Fazekas

The Groot Letaba River is a drawcard for thirsty animals, and its sandy river bank is a good place to read the signs of their nocturnal activities.

Letaba Ranch Nature Reserve, in the upper reaches of the Letaba River system north of Phalaborwa, is a 42,000-hectare reserve that shares an unfenced boundary with the Kruger National Park. The reserve is transected by the Groot Letaba and Klein Letaba rivers. Most of the reserve is owned by the Limpopo Provincial Government, with some parts of it in community ownership. Travelling time from Johannesburg to the reserve is about six hours.

With no public access gate to the Kruger Park for some 150 kilometres between Phalaborwa and Punda Maria gates, the area is quiet and feels off-grid. Indeed, there is only one overnight facility in the reserve, the walks-focused Mtomeni Safari Camp. The camp is part of the African Ivory Route, a cultural and ecotourism initiative that connects several remote camps in the Limpopo region. The nearest shopping opportunity is at Phalaborwa, a 90-minute drive from the reserve gate.

The dominant vegetation south of the Groot Letaba River combines mixed mopane and combretum woodlands. Except for that river system, almost all of the other drainage lines are ephemeral. The grazer population includes healthy numbers of buffalo, zebra, wildebeest and hippo. There are a good number of browsers including giraffe, eland and kudu, while the mixed feeders include elephant and impala. The elusive Sharpe's grysbok is sometimes seen during the winter months. Two packs of African wild dogs frequent the area, and the tracks of vehicle-shy big cats are often found on foot, while the birding along the river is very good.

WALKING IN LETABA RANCH NATURE RESERVE

Although trails are available all year round, the eastern Limpopo region can be exceedingly hot in summer, so the preferred season is April to September. Walking visitors have the option of walks based at African Ivory Route's fixed camp at Mtomeni, or a number of wild-camping trail options with the Spirited Adventures company.

MTOMENI SAFARI CAMP

Overlooking the Groot Letaba River, Mtomeni is a comfortable but not luxury camp. Named for the jackalberry trees that shade the tents, it has eleven units: tents on decks with en-suites that include flush toilets. There's no camp fence, and only solar power for water heating and device charging. Guests may choose self-catered or catered options at the time of booking.

▦ Walk type	Day walk
▦ Booking	www.africanivoryroute.co.za
▦ Cost category	Under R1,500
▦ Group size	2–8
▦ Min. age	14
▦ Season	January–December

Dawn walks from the camp follow the banks of the perennial Groot Letaba, or divert into mopane woodlands to seek out koppies, and cover up to 12 kilometres over three to four hours. A game-viewing vehicle is also available to start walks at remoter locations. For more intensive walking, it's possible to request a three-night wilderness trail experience.

Luiz Otto

Trail guides make sure guests maintain a safe distance from a small group of bachelor buffalo.

Lost spirits of the lowveld

Lutz Otto

Contemplating the lie of the land before the walk starts.

It was the 'blue hour' on the Limpopo coast, that ethereal time between sunset and blackness, and from my vantage point above the beach I gazed out on an ocean that faded in shades of green to the horizon, where it blended with a purple sky. Wait, I hear you say – the Limpopo what now? We know climate change is real, but surely that province doesn't have a coast yet! That's true, but to me it seemed like a sea. I'd travelled far by land through farms and dorps, passing telecoms masts and wire fences, grumbling buses and bullet-riddled road signs. Then, the northern Drakensberg Mountains fell away behind, and the ocean began – the lowveld, South Africa's wild east.

My beach was the sandy shore of a river, where our tents glowed, each a different colour. For me, the wilderness is like the sea because it's a little scary in its otherness, so untouched and unknowable. Sitting in the gathering darkness I wondered what creatures live there undisturbed, remote from the messy human world. There is no better way to discover than to dive beneath the surface. And walking is to the bushveld as scuba diving is to the ocean. So, on foot it would be.

Our voyage of discovery began on the lower Groot Letaba River, before it merges with the Klein Letaba and enters the Kruger National Park to the east. The Letaba Ranch Reserve is little visited compared to its big neighbour, and as the name suggests it was formerly home to more domestic beasts than wild ones. But in recent years the provincial government and community owners have joined the welcome trend of Greater Kruger reserves dropping fences with the national park, allowing the vegetation to regain its natural state and wildlife to return to its natural east-west migration pattern.

A handful of concessions are now responsible for proving that such land can be more beneficial for tourism than for livestock and hunting uses. We gathered and camped the first night near Mtomeni Safari Camp, an outpost of the African Ivory Route company which is a base for vehicle and walking safaris. For this expedition our group was in the care of Spirited Adventures, under the captaincy of Lutz Otto, assisted by Colin Patrick. These two have

We set up our second camp in the shade of a bushveld saffron tree.

thousands of hours logged between them, and as well as bush knowledge they share the farmer's tan of those who spend more of their life outside than indoors, and a disdain for experiencing nature in the cage of a vehicle. Apart from our two veld-seadogs, the group was all female, a sisterhood of serendipity from all corners of the country and beyond.

We spent four nights under canvas, backpacking everything we needed. This meant a heavy pack, even when the non-essentials had been discarded to remain in the vehicle. Lutz knows that the key to enjoying backpacking, especially for first-timers, is thoughtful preparation, and carrying just the essentials and perhaps one or two comfort items.

Before we set out he gifted each of us a buff, that versatile bushveld bandana – it screens the dust when driving in an open vehicle, protects the neck or head from the sun's glare, and can be used to mop the sweat at a rest stop, or wash the body in a bucket shower.

For three days (and a bit) we wandered, adrift. Our serpentine route took us in the footprints of elephants and hippos, along beaches of hot sand and to the top of leopards' koppies. At times I felt we were lost, but had confidence that the navigator knew where we were. Lutz laughed when I asked. 'No, we're not lost,' he said. 'But it happens, it's part of learning and any guide who says they never got lost has not walked enough.' Lutz is sceptical of using GPS devices. Not that he's a technophobe, but he says that they can lead to over-reliance on technology, and the dulling of traditional bush navigation skills.

As he spoke, we were examining where the ground had been disturbed next to a termite hill. Lutz and Colin were like detectives at a murder scene. 'Look, you can see the pattern of the skin,' said Colin, pointing to a depression in the sand. 'And over here, you can touch his tail.' Without knowing it, we were absorbing tracker skills, and in our minds we could now see the elephant at rest, twitching its tail at the flies.

We visitors always want to see the animals themselves, but to a tracker, the recent spoor of an animal is just as real. Colin told me how his kids get this. When he asks them what they saw in the bush, they will reel off the names – lion and cheetah, elephant and buffalo, giraffe, hyena. They mean that they found the tracks, scat and even the animals' scent, proof of their passing. This is the essence of walking in these wild areas, feeling that we are part of nature, knowing the animals are present but not disturbing them.

Lutz knows where to find the line between a pleasant challenge and discomfort. As we relaxed for lunch in the shade of a bushveld saffron tree, he decided it would be a good camping spot, so we left the backpacks there and explored for the afternoon with just day packs. 'The most important thing is that people enjoy it,' said Lutz, reassuring us that the walk experience wasn't meant to be a military ordeal. Maybe it was a concession to the all-female group, but each night he rigged a bucket shower from a tree at a discreet distance, so that we could enjoy a proper wash before the cooking started. I was very happy with this arrangement, as when we'd gone to the Letaba to fetch water we'd scared a few crocodiles off the banks into the river.

Grabbing a moment to update my diary.

As the days passed, our packs grew lighter and my shoulder aches faded. On the last evening we set camp under a grove of jackalberry trees and chilled to the bass sounds of hippo pods. We had fun starting a fire the traditional way, taking turns to spin a twig in a piece of timber, letting hot ashes fall onto dry elephant dung. At last a glow of red appeared, and with some dry grass a fire was blazing on the beach. Still, it was hard work, and I'll continue to pack my Bic lighter in my trail kit.

Later that evening, as the last embers crumbled to ash, we reclined in silence, reading the starscape. No, we were never really lost. And what had we found? Time to think. The serenity of nature. An awareness of our physical capacity. And the value of leaving space for wilderness – it's good for the spirit. **HM**

Lutz Otto

A combination of solid scientific knowledge and boundless curiosity are the hallmark of veteran trail guides such as Jo Watt (left).

SPIRITED ADVENTURES

Spirited Adventures is run by veteran trail guides and the company is committed to providing walking experiences that have zero ecological impact. As well as offering hikes in Letaba Ranch Nature Reserve, guides take trails into the Associated Private Nature Reserves to the south. The company also offers customised trail experiences, from backpacking to slack-packing, with walkers spending three (or more) nights camping wild. Trails are offered year-round, including in the hot summer months. Unusually, Spirited Adventures runs women-only trails, and guiding in German is possible for all German-speaking groups.

■ Walk types	Wilderness trail, backpacking trail
■ Booking	www.spiritedadventures.co.za
■ Cost category	Under R1,500
■ Group size	2–8
■ Min. age	14
■ Season	January–December

For backpacking, hikers need to be totally self-sufficient and fit enough to carry 10–14-kilogram packs in hot conditions. Water is sourced by digging in drainage lines, and purification drops should be used. Having the right kit – and not bringing too much – is key to enjoying backpacking. The company runs regular information meetings in Johannesburg to advise hikers on how to prepare, pack and dress for bushveld expeditions.

Typically, a Spirited Adventures backpack trail covers about 35 kilometres, exploring the river systems of the reserve. As it's a long drive to Letaba Ranch for most guests, it's possible to arrive the night before and camp wild with one of the guides, by arrangement. After meeting at Mtomeni Camp on the first morning, the group transfers by game-viewing vehicle to the trail start. On the final day, everyone is back at base camp by 11:00. Depending on the group and the conditions, the camp either moves to a different site each night or may stay in a certain area, to enable some easier exploration unencumbered by full backpacks.

A good alternative to backpacking, especially in summer, is to take the easier option of a fixed wilderness trail. In this case walkers just need to carry a day pack, and sleep in roomy tents supplied by the company. There's also a slackpacking option, where the camp is packed up each day for relocation by vehicle as walkers explore the terrain.

10 ▪ MAPUNGUBWE NATIONAL PARK

Denis Costello

Situated in a remote corner in the extreme north of South Africa, Mapungubwe National Park's distinctive terrain has much to offer walkers.

In north-western Limpopo, tucked up against the borders of Botswana and Zimbabwe, Mapungubwe National Park has some of the most scenic walking of any park in South Africa. In 2003, Mapungubwe was declared a UNESCO World Heritage Site for its cultural value. Its renowned hill, for which the park is named, is topped with Iron Age ruins from the Mapungubwe Kingdom (c.1075–1220), and near the park entrance is an interesting museum.

   The park is a compact 28,000 hectares in size; fenced private reserves occur on the boundaries, and there are plans to cooperate internationally through the Greater Mapungubwe Transfrontier Conservation Area.

   The terrain is characterised by numerous baobab trees, as well as fever trees and fig trees that grow close to the rivers. Visitors are likely to spot elephant, giraffe, zebra, hyrax and sable antelopes. Animals – including cattle from the communal lands in Zimbabwe – roam freely through the Limpopo River across the international frontier. Mapungubwe National Park is a six-hour drive from Johannesburg, and is one hour west of Musina. Roads in the area are often potholed; drivers should allow extra time for the journey.

WALKING IN MAPUNGUBWE NATIONAL PARK

Mapungubwe has a desert-type climate and is very hot in the summer months, with temperatures averaging in the mid-30s and peaking in the low 40s Celsius. In theory there should be rainfall in the summer, but the area has suffered a prolonged drought. As elsewhere in the Limpopo province, the best walking months are April to September.

SANParks is the only walks operator in the park, and offers interesting early morning explorations, as well as a heritage tour to Mapungubwe Hill, which involves larger groups climbing the hill to learn about the area's history and view the thirteenth-century ruins excavated on the hill's plateau. It's not possible to book Mapungubwe walks online, and it is best to phone in advance to make a booking.

While in the park, be sure to take the Treetop Walk, a boardwalk with views of the Limpopo River. A few kilometres further east there is a short walk to a series of lookouts overlooking the confluence of the Limpopo and Shashe rivers, best visited in the late afternoon as the sun sinks into the haze over Botswana.

Further east again is a camp variously described as Vhembe Trails Camp, Vhembe Wilderness Camp and Vhembe Bush Camp. The different names perhaps reflect its history. The original idea was that it would operate as a base for trail walks like the iMfolozi or Kruger wilderness trails, but this plan didn't get traction. Today Vhembe is one of three camps operated in the park by SANParks, in addition to a six-bed lodge and a camping site.

Dawn walks

Walk type	Day walk
Booking	www.sanparks.org
Cost category	Under R1,500
Group size	2–8
Min. age	12
Season	January–December

Denis Costello

San art can be seen in some rock shelters.

The eastern section of the park is where walks are guided amidst heavily eroded sandstone hills, with views down to the floodplains of the Limpopo River. Dawn walks meet at the park entrance at 06:30, and last about three hours. A snack and fruit juice are provided. Although there is big game present, these walks focus on the plant life, including sculptural Transvaal sesame bushes and stands of lala palms, which grow here at the southern edge of their range. These both lend a tropical ambience to the terrain. Elephants find the fruit of the lala tasty, and palm swifts favour it for nesting. The park guides share their knowledge of plant uses for traditional medicine and as food sources. There's also a chance to examine San rock art in overhangs, and Iron Age stone ruins.

For as long as the sun's heat is low-angled, it's excellent walking terrain, with vantage points to be reached on koppies and rocky ridges. As there's little shade while walking, the aim is to be back at the vehicle before the heat of the day.

Feeling the heat in Limpopo

Johannes Masalesa and Cedric Sethlako are trail guides in Mapungubwe National Park, and they make quite a team. Usually, they take visitors up onto Mapungubwe Hill to tell stories of the rich cultural history of the region. But I'd asked them to take me for a longer walk to explore this stunningly lovely park, and they seemed delighted to compete to share their knowledge of every plant, insect, track and dropping.

Mapungubwe's terrain is highly photogenic, with eroded sandstone hills dropping to the floodplain of the Limpopo River. There's a great diversity of trees: elegant fever trees, huge nyala trees and fine figs. But the eye is always drawn to the many baobabs, now bare without leaves or fruit, sleeping until the rains come. Except for one, which was in full leaf. Cedric explained how this one was lucky to find a water source. Pointing at some artfully constructed buffalo weaverbird nests, he told me how to use the tree as a compass – the birds favour the shadier western side.

Because it has 'buffalo' in its name, this weaver is sometimes listed as one of Africa's Small 5, a playful way to encourage us to look beyond the big animals. Although Mapungubwe does indeed feature the Big 5, one of the pleasures of walking is seeking the smaller things, and my guides were happy to oblige, showing me the trap of the larvae of an antlion, another on the Small 5 list.

Near a huge baobab, trail guides Johannes Masalesa (centre) and Cedric Sethlako (right) told me how these ancient trees are at risk from climate change.

Denis Costello

We climbed a koppie to scan for wildlife. Not far away, a lone bull elephant was busy attacking a young Transvaal sesame bush to get at its nutritious roots. This deep-rooted plant is also food for zebra and kudu, and thrives in arid conditions. Another eye-catching plant here is the lala palm, and Johannes told me how useful it is, a source of materials for mats, hats, bangles and brooms, while the fruit can be eaten or fermented to make palm wine.

Denis Costello

Baobabs have evolved to survive elephant damage.

We watched some dassies – hyrax, or *imbila* in SiSwati – soaking up the sun, and Cedric and I remembered the children's story about how their laziness led to the lack of a tail. *Imbila yeswela umsila ngekulayetela* – the dassie had no tail because when the animals were called to receive their tails, the dassie told a friend to bring one for him and stayed lazing on his rock. But the tails had all been given out before the friend could get one.

Johannes and Cedric led me to an overhang to show me some San rock art, little human figures in ochre red. It was not hard to imagine the artists lingering here in the heat of the day, telling stories of dassies. When we stepped into the sun again, a klipspringer danced away up a rock face. It was also time for us to escape. There seemed to be a switch flicked at nine o'clock that changed the air temperature from comfortable to excessively hot. I asked Cedric when the best time of year is to visit Mapungubwe, if there is a cooler time. He chuckled and said it's always hot, and sometimes hotter. But you can tell he and Johannes love the place.

Before leaving the park, I drove to the Limpopo River and took the Treetop Walk, a raised boardwalk with views of Botswana and Zimbabwe. A herd of cows was slowly making its way into the park from the Zimbabwe side – a bone of contention, as the park's vegetation is already looking well chowed by wildlife. There are plans to expand the park and make it a true transfrontier reserve. It would be wonderful if in the future we could roam as freely as those cows. With its prolific birdlife, beautiful trees and interesting topography, it would be ideal for more walks. Before nine, at least. **HM**

Denis Costello

A close encounter with rhino in the dense bush of Marakele National Park is not unusual.

The Waterberg region, a malaria-free area with easy access from the large population centres in Gauteng, is a popular bush escape. Located in the west of Limpopo, it's one of South Africa's most scenic regions, a dramatic landscape of escarpments overlooking sandveld, sourveld and wetlands. In 2001 the Waterberg was designated a UNESCO Biosphere Reserve, with a core area of over 100,000 hectares and a buffer zone of 185,000 hectares.

In the south-west of the Waterberg massif, three hours from Johannesburg, Marakele National Park is a relatively new reserve established as a national park in 1994. It has since grown to over 67,000 hectares. The terrain is a visually pleasing mix of bushveld plains backed by sandstone peaks of over 2,000 metres. The drive to Lenong Lookout, via a tarred road, is a highlight of any visit, and there's a good chance of encountering elephants on the twisting road, so drivers should take care at corners.

Other big game encountered at Marakele Park includes black and white rhino, buffalo, giraffe and lion. It's a good place to spot many species of mountain-loving antelope, including klipspringer, mountain reedbuck and grey rhebok. The rich birdlife includes a large colony of Cape vultures that nest on the cliffs below Lenong.

WALKING IN MARAKELE NATIONAL PARK

Marakele has a warm, temperate climate and the summer months from November to February have the highest rainfall, which often comes in the form of thunderstorms. Walking is possible year-round, but it's better late in the season, when the bush has thinned – August to October being best of all, with less chance of rain and pleasant daytime temperatures. April and May are also good months to visit, and it gets cold at night in June and July. Summer walking can also be enjoyable, but the bushveld can be dense at this time of year.

SANParks offers accommodation at Bontle Rest Camp and Tlopi Tented Camp; both camps are suited to self-catering, as there is no shop or restaurant in the park. In 2020, a SANParks Honorary Rangers (SHR) rustic bush camp was established in the western sector of the reserve as a base for wilderness trails. Marakele is also home to a private concession with a strong walking safari focus, the luxury Marataba Lodges operated by the MORE Family Collection. All three of these organisations offer year-round trail walking.

Outside Marakele, much of the Waterberg Biosphere is conserved in privately owned lands, including the Welgevonden Game Reserve that shares a boundary with the park, with SANParks and Welgevonden owners hoping to reach an agreement to remove the fencing in the future. Both Welgevonden and Entabeni Safari Conservancy to the east have wildlife populations that include elephant, rhino, giraffe, zebra, lion, wildebeest, hippo and many species of antelope. These two reserves contain private lodges with trail guides, and walks are available on request.

Day walks

Lit by a rising sun, Marakele's sandstone cliffs offer a stunning backdrop to the morning walks operated by SANParks. There are various starting points, but it's usual to drive from the camp reception to the eastern sector of the park where elephant, rhino and buffalo roam. There, the bushveld is dominated by small-leafed thorny species and can be dense, so it's important that group members stay close together. As the land rises, the predominant vegetation type is Waterberg moist mountain bushveld. Where possible, the trails explore sandy watercourses amidst copses of fig trees, ironwood and waterberry. Overhead there is invariably the silhouette of a Cape vulture or other raptor, with 44 species listed for the park.

Guests should contact the park in advance of travel to establish whether a trail guide will be available to lead a walk. Although afternoon walks may be listed on the SANParks website, they weren't operating at the time of writing due to a shortage of guides.

Walk type	Day walk
Booking	www.sanparks.org
Cost category	Under R1,500
Group size	4–8
Min. age	12
Season	January–December

Denis Costello

The landscape makes for a dramatic sunset.

Trailing the trainee trail guides

It is not that Marakele National Park is any more spikey than other parks, but that evening, after a day with a group of trainee trail guides, some work was needed to extract all the acacia thorns from the soles of my boots. The trainees were being assessed in the field and their instructors deliberately led us into thick thornveld, to maximise the possibility of close and unexpected contacts with dangerous animals. Each such encounter is logged by the trainee, with 50 required before qualification as an apprentice trail guide. Me, I learned a new skill – how to reverse into a thorn bush and use my backpack as a shield.

Leading walkers in areas with big game is not something to be taken lightly, and the standard of trail guides in South African parks is world-class, thanks to rigorous training programmes and certification. The trainees were following courses administered by the Field Guides Association of Southern Africa (see pages 28–29). Several private companies provide the training, and our group was led by Sakkie van Aswegen from Bushveld Training Adventures, a highly regarded expert in bushcraft. We set off with Jan-Hendrik Pieters, from Entabeni Safari Conservancy, whose guiding was being assessed during the trail. He carried a rifle, unloaded. At the front, Sakkie and his assistant, Marius Ferreira, kept watch over Jan-Hendrik, and also kept a lookout for animals that might be hidden in the thick bush ahead. Two more armed rangers followed the group for additional safety.

It was a fascinating glimpse into the process of becoming a trail guide. The field test is more of a mental challenge than a physical one. I had

Denis Costello

A scratching post provided an opportunity for the trainees to share their knowledge.

recently gained my driving licence, and found the test a nerve-jangling experience. But it was as nothing compared to what Jan-Hendrik must have been feeling. When moving, he had to concentrate his senses to perceive animals ahead, not easy in the strong wind. In that area of Marakele there were elephant, buffalo and rhino, and if we met one at close quarters, he had to be ready to show the correct response and keep the group safe.

When we paused, Jan-Hendrik had to field all sorts of questions, and I played my part by asking as many as I could. The subjects ranged widely. Elephant eyes – did you know they have a 'third eyelid' that moves vertically across the eye? How to tell the track of a female lion from those of a small male. The ossicones of the giraffe and how they help cushion a calf's fall during birth. We paused to examine a kudu skull. The enormous horns of the male are a hindrance when attacked by a predator, getting caught in the trees. Communicating clear information to a group of walkers without raising your voice is a skill in itself.

After a couple of hours, we took a break and I chatted with the trainees. I found a wide span of ages and motivations for taking the training among them. Marjone Enslin was the only female trainee, and still in her teens. She grew up on a game farm, and was now looking to deepen her knowledge and learn how to share it with others. All were already volunteering as SANParks Honorary Rangers, and planned to work as guides in national parks or in one of the many private reserves in the Waterberg area.

We walked for about five hours, longer than a normal guided walk. It was never dull, and the other trainees were happy to show their knowledge. One of the pleasures of walking in South African parks is the lifelong opportunity to learn about nature, with a new experience always around the next tree. For me, the highlight was finding a trove of broken dung beetle larval cases, excavated by a honey badger. 'No, by a ratel,' insisted Sakkie. He said the common English name leads people to the false belief that they are a relative of the badger.

Denis Costello

A highlight of the walk was finding broken dung beetle larval cases, excavated by a ratel.

A little later we found a perfect polished scratching post, and the chat ranged over animal parasites, and the properties of elephant and rhino skin. Somehow, we then moved on to talk about animal night vision, and how the *tapetum lucidum* – the reflective layer in the eye of cats and dogs – works. We met a couple of elephants busy feeding, and Jan-Hendrik was happy to log another encounter. It was not until we were back in sight of the camp that we had our best big animal sighting – two rhinos, very close. We followed the guide's hand gestures, and safely passed them. **HM**

Denis Costello

Navigating the thornveld
requires patience.

SANPARKS HONORARY RANGERS

■ Walk type	Wilderness trail
■ Booking	www.sanparksvolunteers.org
■ Cost category	Under R1,500
■ Group size	6–8
■ Min. age	12
■ Season	February–November

The SANParks Honorary Rangers (SHR) runs a rustic camping experience in the Zandfontein/ Ditabaneng area of Marakele National Park, west of the Rooiberg Road (also locally called Hoopdal Road). It began operating in 2020 and is modelled on the SHR Nyarhi Rustic Bush Camp in the Kruger Park (see page 107), giving small groups the rare opportunity to spend two nights in the wild, off-grid and unfenced, with minimal impact on the environment.

Known as Morukuru, the Tswana name for the tamboti tree, the camp is located in a shady grove in an area of sandveld and mixed bushveld that is habitat for rhino, leopard and plains game, including giraffe, zebra, wildebeest, nyala, kudu and smaller antelope. There are plans to remove the fencing along the Rooiberg Road, which will allow elephant, buffalo and lion to access the area.

As at Nyarhi, camp facilities are minimal, and guests need to be self-sufficient in all respects, bringing their own tent or off-road caravan, food, utensils, refrigeration, camping stoves and camp furniture. Guests should also bring sufficient water for washing, cooking and drinking. The camp facilities comprise Enviro Loos, shower screens, and a braai pit and grid. Firewood is supplied, but there's no harm in bringing some extra wood along.

After settling into camp on the first day, members of the group can explore the area on a short walk. The activities of the second and third days are determined by the wishes and abilities of the group. A typical day would see participants set off with two guides shortly after dawn, returning to camp in the early afternoon. Everyone carries their own water and snacks for breakfast and lunch. The walks cross into the big game section of the park, where the aim is to explore the attractive gorges and kloofs, watching for wildlife and stopping to investigate smaller flora and fauna. There are also opportunities to cool off in pools during the warmer months. After a convivial evening swapping stories around the campfire, guests retire to sleep amidst the nocturnal music of nature. Dates for when Morukuru Rustic Bush Camp is operational are announced on the SHR website. It's available on a group-booking basis for a maximum of eight people per group, and guests meet the rangers at the park reception before driving to the campsite.

MORE Family Collection

Some Marataba walks explore dramatic and picturesque gorges.

MARATABA TRAILS

The MORE Family Collection operates two high-end lodges (Marataba Safari Lodge and Marataba Mountain Lodge) in a 23,000-hectare contractual park that comprises the northern third of Marakele National Park. It's one of the most luxurious and expensive concessions in South Africa, and very welcoming to walkers. From the lodges, walks of 1.5 to 2 hours are possible every day, but three times a week the Marataba Trails experience sees guests guided on more challenging three- to four-hour walks. The maximum group size is usually six, but can be increased to eight if the planned route is not too challenging. Walks are for overnight guests only, and should be requested at the time of booking. Walking activities involve an additional fee.

Walk type	Day walk
Booking	www.marataba.co.za
Cost category	Over R6,000
Group size	2–6
Min. age	16
Season	January–December

The walks make the most of the contrasting range of terrains in Marakele National Park. Some stay low, tracking rivers and waterholes, while others penetrate the mountains in narrow gorges, with the reward of pools for a cooling dip. The most challenging walks ascend the mountains. There are also sites of historical interest in the trails area, including San rock art, Stone Age artefacts and Iron Age ruins.

The group meets at either of the lodges at 06:00 in summer and 07:00 in winter for transfer by game-viewing vehicle to the starting point. Water and snacks are provided. There are also day packs to borrow if guests need these. Each walk is led by two experienced guides, who have been trained at the nearby NJ More Field Guide College. While mainly focused on training professionals, the college also offers an Adventure Course for the general public, with participants based at a tented camp with comfortable facilities, including electricity and en suites. For more information about the course, see www.njmorefieldguidecollege. co.za Contact details are: tel: +27 (0) 87 980 4144; email: francois@more.co.za

flowcomm/Flickr

Lucky visitors might spot Rain, a female cheetah that has raised four cubs to independence.

In North West Province, just a two-hour drive from Pretoria, the 55,000-hectare Pilanesberg Game Reserve is smaller and busier than Marakele National Park and contains a wide range of southern African wildlife, including lion and cheetah, elephant, rhino, hippo, buffalo, African wild dog, hyena and prolific birdlife. The circular shape of the present park reflects the area's origins as a large volcanic caldera, and results in an interesting topography that contrasts with the mostly flat terrain of the province.

Pilanesberg is sometimes referred to as a national park, but that is for historical reasons, and it does not actually have that status. It is owned and managed by the North West Parks and Tourism Board and, unlike SANParks, the board does not operate camps or take bookings directly. Instead there are lodges run by private concessions within the park, while the large Sun City Resort is adjacent, with other resorts on the fringes.

WALKING IN PILANESBERG GAME RESERVE

Walks are available year-round in the Pilanesberg Game Reserve, and are more comfortable in the cooler season from April to September. Walking is not a major activity, but as the reserve allows self-drive, wildlife sightings can be busy, so walks offer a pleasant and quieter alternative.

There are two main options for accessing trails. The first is to contact the Mankwe Gametrackers company, which operates game drives and ballooning in Pilanesberg and can also facilitate bush walks, picking up guests at any Sun City hotel or at the gates of

Andre van Rensburg, head guide at Bakubung Bush Lodge, takes time out to survey the landscape.

the Bakubung Complex, Manyane Resort and Ivory Tree Lodge. Walks are open to those aged 16 to 75; they start at 06:00–06:30 and last about four hours. Water is provided, but guests should bring their own snacks. See www.mankwegametrackers.co.za for more information about these walks.

The second and recommended option is to book into either of the two larger Legacy Hotel Group bush lodges, Kwa Maritane or Bakubung, both in attractive locations deep in the park. These lodges offer dawn walks to their guests throughout the year.

LEGACY HOTELS

Both Legacy Hotel bush lodges in the Pilanesberg Game Reserve have qualified trail guides on their staff and offer dawn walks of three to five hours. They depart at times from 05:30 to 07:00, depending on the season. Walks are provided at an additional fee and a breakfast pack is included, with sandwiches, fruit, chocolate, juice and water.

The walks operate throughout the year unless conditions are not suitable, such as in case of rain or when long grass increases the risks. One guide is used for groups of up to four, and two guides if there are more guests. The maximum age for walkers is surprisingly low at 60.

The Pilanesberg is in the transition zone between the arid Kalahari Desert and the greener bushveld of the Waterberg, and walking there is an opportunity to learn why the area is special, and how its geology and terrain influence the flora and fauna that occur there.

Walk type	Day walk
Booking	www.legacyhotels.co.za
Cost category	R1,500–R3,000
Group size	2–8
Min. age	16
Season	January–December

13 ▪ KGALAGADI TRANSFRONTIER PARK

Denis Costello

The grassy dunes of the Kgalagadi Park may look barren but are rich in flora and fauna.

The Kalahari Desert is a place apart, a treeless landscape famous for big cat sightings, sometimes close up in the unfenced camps. With the Botswana side included, the Kgalagadi Transfrontier Park protects 3,6 million hectares of land, which exceeds all the other reserves in this book combined. In the past, the vegetation supported low numbers of elephant, hippo and rhino, but these animals are long gone. Even without these bigger animals, the park has a wealth of wildlife including herds of springbok and gemsbok, leopard, hyena and cheetah.

The park is wonderfully remote, with the entrance gate almost three hours' drive from Upington in the Northern Cape. It's hot and exposed, and best suited to a leisurely exploration by 4×4, but there are opportunities to move around on foot amidst the grassy dunes.

WALKING IN THE KGALAGADI TRANSFRONTIER PARK

The Kgalagadi Transfrontier Park has a desert climate; it is mostly dry, but rain may fall in summer, usually during occasional thunderstorms. The heat is excessive in mid-summer, averaging 35°C and often rising above 40°C, but early morning temperatures are fine for the sort of walks on offer. Late March to early May is an ideal time to visit. Then, the heat has eased, and any rain that might have fallen would have resulted in the greening of the grasslands and the blooming of desert flowers. The midwinter months from June to August are cold at night, and even frosty. September and October are also good months to visit, with the weather warming and the night skies clear.

There are five national parks and a number of other reserves in the vast, arid and sparsely populated Northern Cape. Many of these offer wonderful walking opportunities, but it is only the Kgalagadi Transfrontier Park that requires guides because of the presence of predators, particularly lions. Walking in the Kgalagadi is quite different to walking in the other parks covered in this guide. The treeless dunes and year-round heat make it impossible to offer the types of trails available in other parts of South Africa. There are no multi-day walks, and although SANParks experimented with a trail camp in the past, it was discontinued as the environment is simply not suitable – it's too sandy and too hot.

Nevertheless, it's rewarding to explore the terrain on foot when possible, as there is a rich diversity of desert plants, birds, insects and rodents. In the past, the SANParks camps at Twee Rivieren and Nossob offered guided morning and afternoon walks, but a shortage of trail guides has seen these walks discontinued at the time of writing. It's worth enquiring about them at the park reception – if there's visitor demand, perhaps they will resume. Only one place in the park offers guided walks, !Xaus Lodge.

!XAUS LODGE

!Xaus Lodge is on the south-west boundary of the park, a three-hour drive from the park entrance and main rest camp at Twee Rivieren. Access is strictly by 4×4, and guests can be met and transferred from Kamqua Picnic Site to the lodge. There is sheltered parking near Kamqua for guest vehicles. This private concession is owned by the local ‡Khomani San community, and managed on their behalf by a not-for-profit company. The San guides speak English and Afrikaans as well as their own language. The walks provide an opportunity to learn from descendants of Africa's earliest inhabitants, who have a continuous history of survival in one of the earth's harshest terrains.

Walks don't cover long distances, and the emphasis is on learning about the flora, smaller fauna and traditional lore. Almost every plant has a craft, cultural, food or medicinal use for the San. Walks can be taken at dawn or before sunset, and are included in the overnight fees.

While staying at !Xaus Lodge, a night drive is highly recommended, and guests are likely to spot African wild cat, hyena, bat-eared fox, spring hare and spotted eagle owl. A craft kraal next to the lodge provides an opportunity for guests to witness and try their hand at the creation of traditional San jewellery and carvings.

Walk type	Day walk
Booking	www.xauslodge.co.za
Cost category	R1,500–R3,000
Group size	1–8
Min. age	12
Season	January–December

The chalets of !Xaus Lodge overlook a pan.

The pharmacy of the dunes

Denis Costello

Guide Mans Maasdorp identified a few seedpods that are useful to the San.

Kek kek kek kek. 'That's the sound of spring in the Kalahari,' said my guide. It's the call of the male barking gecko doing its utmost to attract a female to its burrow, and it seemed to follow us around. My guide was Mans Maasdorp, and he may have been born in Upington but you could tell that his heart is here in the arid lands north of the Orange River. We were in the Kgalagadi Transfrontier Park and exploring the dunes near !Xaus Pan. The name means 'heart' in the Nama (or Khoekhoe) language, because of its shape.

Another sound rumbled from the near distance. 'Is that a lion?' I asked him. Mans said yes, and explained that a male lion had killed a gemsbok on the other side of the pan and had been feeding for a few days. 'Some people mix up the sounds of the ostrich and the lion,' he explained, before doing a good imitation of each call. He told me not to worry about the lion. 'We avoid them, and they avoid us.'

We went back to examining the dunes, which were bathed in early morning light. This was not the bare red sand I'd imagined. Mans said that dunes without grass are the result of overgrazing. Protected in the enormous park, these dunes are rich in plant life, and host to thriving populations of rodents and reptiles, birds and mammals.

A million tiny tracks dappled the sand in signature patterns: rodents, skinks, beetles, scorpions, Namaqua doves. My eyes followed a minuscule trail around a colourful clump of wild everlasting, and led me to a chubby rodent, a whistling rat, hanging out at the mouth of a burrow. He was not alone, but these creatures are well camouflaged and hard to spot until they move. In a similar way, the four-striped grass mice like to stay still when approached. They use the blackthorn bushes as a natural defence against predators such as wild cats and birds. Mans said that even kudus can reverse into a blackthorn if threatened by a lion, the barbed thorns forming a good barrier.

Denis Costello

I watched Mans excavating tubers of devil's claw.

Mans was happy to talk geckos and rodents, but he really got into his stride when telling me about the useful plants in this environment, a veritable pharmacy of the dunes. The devil's claw plant doesn't look like much, but it's a proven source of anti-rheumatic and anti-inflammatory medicines. Mans dug out the tubers by hand. Nearby, a buffalo thorn was not just a home for sociable weaver nests, but a source of berries to make alcohol, while the roots can be used for stomach ailments.

We moved on, our hands brushing stiff clumps of grass, making an oceanic sound. Mans said the local name for this plant is gami grass, from the Nama word for water. He pointed out the different types of grasses. Some, called eragrostis, are perennial, others he calls 'one-year grasses'. A little further on, Mans stopped at a small succulent and broke off a stem. 'This is the candle bush, because when it's dry we use it as a candle,' he said. 'How do you light it?', I asked. 'With one of these,' replied Mans with a smile, pulling a Bic lighter from his pocket.

On the second morning at the most comfortable !Xaus Lodge, I woke to the sound of the lion at close quarters. I found him drinking from the water trough in the pan, 80 metres from the chalet. When feeding, they need to come to drink often. His presence nearby did not deter us from going for another walk, as a member of staff was charged with keeping an eye on him, and Mans carried a two-way radio.

Mans had not run out of interesting facts to share. We started by looking for the local meerkat family, but they were staying underground. Then Mans gathered a selection of seed pods from camelthorn and other

Denis Costello

Mans explains the intricacies of a large sociable weaver nest in a buffalo thorn tree.

trees. Later I was to see how the San fashion these into attractive items of jewellery. And they use blackthorn wood to make walking and digging sticks and fence poles.

The birds were not ignored. As well as the many weaver birds, we found flocks of red-headed finches, and several southern pale chanting goshawks. The area is popular with ground-dwelling birds, and we spotted the northern black korhaan, kori bustard and ostrich.

The stinking shepherd's bush – called by this name because of its flower's scent – is greatly valued by the San. In December the berries appear, and can be eaten or used to make a sort of yoghurt. The roots of its cousin, the shepherd's tree, can be roasted and ground to brew a coffee substitute. Of course, the name 'shepherd' comes from its shade-giving properties, and Mans claimed that the temperature under its branches can be 20°C lower than in the unshaded area around the tree. Indeed, that afternoon as we went for a drive, we knew exactly where to look for 'our' lion, and found him sprawled belly-up under the shepherd's tree. **HM**

Denis Costello

A lion sprawls under a shepherd's bush.

Although famous for its big cats, the Kgalagadi Transfrontier Park is home to diverse animal life, best appreciated by exploring this fascinating desert wilderness on foot.

Black mamba

African wild cat

Tracks of a corn cricket

Black-backed jackal

Red hartebeest

Steenbok

The stark beauty of Sanbona's arid karooveld is one of this reserve's main attractions.

The only reserve with big game walking opportunities within the proximity of Cape Town is the Sanbona Wildlife Reserve in the Klein Karoo. Like Jock Safari Lodge in the Kruger National Park, it is owned by the not-for-profit Caleo Foundation, and offers a choice of four luxury camps and lodges. It's a 3.5-hour drive from Cape Town, 30 minutes from the town of Montagu, and day visits are not permitted. Sanbona is a big reserve, larger than Mountain Zebra National Park (see chapter 16), and conserves 58,000 hectares of arid karooveld. As this habitat does not support large numbers of grazers, visitors are encouraged to look beyond the big animals and appreciate the whole ecosystem, from geology to plants, insects, birds and the smaller mammals.

WALKING IN SANBONA WILDLIFE RESERVE

The Western Cape is a pleasure to visit in all seasons, with the finest walking in summer. The months from October to December provide the best balance of day and night temperatures, combined with the peak flowering season. High summer is hot by day, and there is little shade in the reserve, but the warm evenings make camping a pleasure. March and April are also good months to visit, while by May the nights are getting cold. The winter months bring chill winds and even snow, so while the walking can be good, it's too cold for camping.

At Sanbona, guests on game drives leave the vehicle at various points for short walks to examine the smaller natural features, including quartz patches and succulent plants. For keen walkers, the reserve operates a highly recommended Explorer Camp wilderness trail through the summer months.

Explorer Camp

■ Walk type	Wilderness trail
■ Booking	www.sanbona.com
■ Cost category	R3,000–R6,000
■ Group size	2–6
■ Min. age	16
■ Season	October–April

Sanbona

Sanbona's comfortable Explorer Camp is newly erected each season.

Sanbona's seasonal Explorer Camp is a wild but comfortable camp with minimal fencing and just three tents. Meals are prepared over an open fire, there is no electricity, and there's a choice of composting toilets or the en-suite chemical toilet for each tent. Each day, walkers are guided on animal tracks for walks of three to four hours, the duration determined according to guests' preference.

The Explorer Camp operates in summer, from October through to April, with a set departure time on a Friday for two nights. It is recommended that walking visitors make a long weekend of their stay by spending two nights in the camp and Sunday at a luxury lodge.

Sanbona

At dusk, the campfire becomes the focus; here, tales of the day's adventures are recounted.

15 ▪ GONDWANA GAME RESERVE

Raquel de Castro Maia

Surrounded by mountains, Gondwana's varied landscape of rolling hills, open plains and deep valleys offers all the ingredients for a rewarding walking safari.

Surrounded by the Langeberg and Outeniqua Mountains, the 11,000-hectare Gondwana Game Reserve is in a prime and accessible position on the Western Cape's Garden Route. The reserve is not far from Mossel Bay and almost 400 kilometres from Cape Town, or about 4.5 hours' driving. It is privately owned, catering for overnight luxury safaris, and day visits are not permitted.

Although it is home to a range of big game, including lion, hippo, elephant, rhino, buffalo and plains animals such as eland, giraffe and zebra, the landscape and flora of the reserve are in great contrast to the lowveld. It's the diversity of plant life that makes walking here unique – Gondwana boasts over 1,000 different species of plant, many of them threatened fynbos species and a few that can only be seen in this reserve and nowhere else in the world. There's something special and colourful flowering in abundance in all seasons. Various species of protea and erica bloom all year round and attract prolific endemic birdlife, and a splendid variety of succulents and renosterveld plants are also found here.

Gondwana's mix of grass plains and fynbos makes for a botanist's paradise, and flowering plants are seen year-round. Below is a small sample of some of the reserve's most conspicuous species.

Leucospermum cuneiforme

Protea neriifolia

Tritonia securigera

Pelargonium cordifolium

Disperis capensis

Lobostemon fruticosus

Freesia fucata

WALKING IN GONDWANA GAME RESERVE

The open grassland and fynbos landscape make Gondwana Game Reserve perfect for summer walking. Although the larger wildlife is best spotted on drives, all visitors are encouraged to accompany experts on guided 'botanical conservation' walks, an opportunity to get up close to the fascinating plant life and learn about the conservation of the rare and endangered fynbos biome. These walks last two to three hours, and are offered daily in the downtime between morning and evening game drives.

In summer, Gondwana offers the Pioneer Trail, a multi-day exploration of the reserve. Small groups walk with two qualified trail guides and overnight in a series of elegant tented camps.

Pioneer Trail

■ Walk type	Wilderness trail	
■ Booking	www.gondwanagr.co.za	
■ Cost category	R3,000–R6,000	
■ Group size	1–8	
■ Min. age	12	
■ Season	September–May	

To really enjoy the reserve on foot, the time to visit is during the summer months from September to May, when Gondwana operates the three-night tented Pioneer Trail in slackpacking style. Departures are on Mondays and Thursdays, and each night is spent in a different unfenced fly camp. It's a fine way to combine bushwalking and learning, with plenty of time left in the afternoons and evenings to relax in a serene natural setting.

Guide Mike Nagel admires a *Brunsvigia josephinae* (above and below). Its enormous flowers are pollinated by sunbirds.

Raquel de Castro Maia

Raquel de Castro Maia

Gondwana's camps don't skimp on creature comforts.

On the first day, trail guests meet their guides at Lehele Lodge in the reserve and take a light lunch. They then sort the kit they need for three nights into the duffle bags provided; their remaining luggage and valuables can be locked in their vehicles. The adventure begins as guests and guides proceed to the first tented camp in an open game-viewing vehicle, taking time to stop for interesting sightings. The aim is to reach the camp by 16:00 for afternoon tea.

At the camps every comfort is provided, with walk-in tents that have proper beds and en-suite facilities. There's a luxury open lounge tent where guests can relax and enjoy the view. Before dinner, the guides give a briefing on the plans for the next day, and the meal is served in a dining tent lit by lanterns. On a clear night, guests can enjoy a splendid starscape.

Breakfast is taken after a gentle wake-up call at 06:00 or 06:30, after which guests repack their duffle bags. By 07:30 everyone is on the trail, carrying only a light day pack with lunch and water. The terrain is undulating, but not overly strenuous. The first walking day covers over 10 kilometres of hilly terrain, at a pace that leaves plenty of time to stop for game sightings and to absorb the expertise of the guides as they reveal the unique flora. The next day's walk is shorter and takes guests into the magnificent Nauga Valley, where there may even be a chance for a wild waterhole swim.

Between 14:00 and 16:00, the group reaches the next camp for welcome refreshments, a wash and a restful afternoon. The third camp is nestled in the heart of the reserve with a great opportunity for game-viewing, so an afternoon game drive is an option.

16 ▪ MOUNTAIN ZEBRA NATIONAL PARK

Denis Costello

SANParks trail guide Richard Okkers leads the ascent of Salpeterkop on a day walk.

A mid-size reserve of 40,000 hectares, Mountain Zebra National Park is in the east of the Great Karoo region and close to the town of Cradock. The main biomes in the reserve are Nama-Karoo, grassland and thicket, and its landscape of volcanic outcrops, deep gullies and varied elevations provides spectacular scenery, while the extensive grasslands make game-viewing easy.

The park is named for the Cape mountain zebra, the locally endangered subspecies that is larger than the common plains zebra. With several hundred of these animals in the park, visitors will be sure to spot them grazing alongside herds of red hartebeest, black wildebeest, blesbok and springbok. Less easy to find are the small populations of lion and black rhino. The park is one of the few places where guests can encounter wild cheetah on foot, by taking part in cheetah tracking walks.

SANParks provides excellent accommodation at the rest camp in the park, which is set attractively on the lower slopes of the 1,200-metre Soetkop, and there are also a couple of mountain cottages and a guest house on the Kranskop loop in the southern section.

WALKING IN MOUNTAIN ZEBRA NATIONAL PARK

The Eastern Cape is a summer walking destination, although these months also bring the highest risk of rainfall, peaking in February and March. At this time of year vegetation growth can be high, making wildlife spotting harder. In the colder winter months from May to September, it's a bit harsh to be out in an open game-viewing vehicle at dawn. On balance, the months of October to January provide the best walking conditions.

SANPARKS WALK EXPERIENCES

There are two signposted walking trails within the fenced Mountain Zebra National Park Rest Camp that can be self-guided. The 1-kilometre Imbila Trail is an easy stroll along flat ground, while the 2,5-kilometre Black Eagle Trail climbs steeply from behind the rest camp to a rocky crag with fine views. In the past, Mountain Zebra had longer self-guided, multi-day trails – Impofu, a three-day, 25-kilometre route, and Idwala, a one-day trail. Sadly, following a fatal buffalo encounter, they closed in 2010. They reopened for a while as ranger-guided trails, but that has been discontinued.

SANParks offers an interesting selection of year-round escorted day walks, covering a diversity of interests from general wildlife to cheetah tracking, South African War remains, rock art and a climb to the park's highest peak. No snacks or water are provided, so walkers should supply their own.

Morning walks

Guided walks depart from the rest camp at 05:00 in summer and 06:30 in winter, and last about three hours. Locations vary, and sometimes part of the 10-kilometre Idwala Trail route is used.

Walkers should be prepared for some steep climbs, but with plenty of stops to admire the views. The dawn walks focus on the park's flora and fauna, and after the walk is over the park operates a Rock Art Walk. This brings visitors to view a number of San cave paintings; it starts at 09:00 and takes two hours. The trail is for the sure-footed, as it requires some navigation over loose rocks. There are three overhangs with painted depictions of humans, baboons and antelopes. Visitors can also look out for mountain reedbuck in this area.

▦ Walk type	Day walk
▦ Booking	www.sanparks.org
▦ Cost category	Under R1,500
▦ Group size	2–9
▦ Min. age	12
▦ Season	January–December

The Mountain Zebra National Park was established to protect the Cape mountain zebra, a species on the brink of extinction by the early 1930s.

Denis Costello

Denis Costello

A number of cheetah in the Mountain Zebra National Park wear radio transmitter collars (above), allowing them to be tracked using radio telemetry (right).

Denis Costello

Cheetah tracking walks

▦ Walk type	Day walk
▦ Booking	www.sanparks.org
▦ Cost category	Under R1,500
▦ Group size	2–8
▦ Min. age	12
▦ Season	January–December

Cheetah tracking is a special experience, and Mountain Zebra is the only national park to offer it. Although associated more with savannah regions than with karooveld, cheetah can be present in all biomes apart from dense forest and at high altitude, and the cats roamed wild here up to the late nineteenth century. They were reintroduced to the park in 2007 as part of a cheetah conservation programme. Some of them have been collared, allowing them to be tracked using radio telemetry. The collars don't interfere with the animals' natural behaviour and enable scientists to monitor their activity.

Unlike other big cats, cheetah quickly become habituated to humans on foot, and it's possible to approach them up to a close distance without causing disturbance. The cheetah in the park are wild animals, living free, and the experience is tightly controlled by SANParks. Several private reserves in South Africa offer similar ethical cheetah tracking experiences on foot, but there are others that are part of the big cat captive breeding industry; anywhere that offers cub-cuddling and selfies should be avoided.

The initial search for the collared animals is vehicle-based, and the group drives around until the guide picks up a signal. Once a cheetah is located, everyone gets down to track it. Depending on how far away from the 4×4 route the cat is, the walk can be anything from 20 minutes to several hours. Typically, the whole experience lasts between three and four hours.

Walks depart at 08:30, and advance bookings are essential. They are not permitted to start earlier (or after 15:00) so as not to disrupt the cheetahs' hunting time.

Salpeterkop Ascent

The peak of Salpeterkop overlooks the northern section of the Mountain Zebra National Park and makes for an interesting half-day walk. The group meets at the rest camp reception at 05:00 in summer and 07:00 in winter.

It takes more than an hour to drive the 4×4 track to the foot of the mountain, and from there it's another 1.5 hours ascending Salpeterkop on a scree trail amidst invasive

Walk type	Day walk
Booking	www.sanparks.org
Cost category	Under R1,500
Group size	2–8
Min. age	12
Season	January–December

prickly pear plants. The climb is worth it for the views, and the relics of the South African War (1899–1902). The area had historical significance as a British lookout point during that war, and some of the soldiers left their mark by carving a chessboard on a flat rock on the summit, along with graffiti of their names and regiments. In all, with stops for game-viewing along the way, the excursion lasts five to six hours.

Denis Costello

A chessboard carved on a rock on the summit of Salpeterkop is a relic of the South African War.

Searching for Mabula

Denis Costello

Mabula, a member of the thriving cheetah population in the Mountain Zebra National Park

It's good manners to stop and admire the zebras in Mountain Zebra National Park. Especially if they are posing nicely on a mountainside in the first sun rays of the day. But I was wrapped in a blanket and impatient: I had a rendezvous with a cheetah. And my confidence about finding one was high, thanks to technology. Two of the cheetah in the park have been collared by researchers, and their location can be tracked with a handheld scanner. How hard could it be?

Quite tricky, in fact. The signals travel by line of sight, and the park – did I mention it has mountains? And valleys, ridges, clefts, gullies, koppies, dongas, thickets. You get the picture. Park guide Richard Okkers was tasked with the tracking, while Desigan Naidoo (known as Desh) showed off his 4×4 driving skills. We turned onto the Rooiplaat Loop road and drove through sweetveld where springbok and eland grazed. Richard got down at a vantage point and lifted his scanner. I heard a steady buzz. 'Nothing here,' he said to Desh. 'Let's try Kranskop.'

When cheetah were reintroduced in 2011 they were top cats in the park and thrived. So much so that over 30 cheetahs have been relocated to other parks and reserves under the Cheetah Metapopulation Project managed by the Endangered Wildlife Trust (EWT). Then, in 2013, lions were also reintroduced, and researchers watched to see how these species would interact.

Despite the cold, part of me was happy that the cheetahs were not easy to find. These are wild animals, with a big territory to roam. Richard told me that sometimes it can be quite a challenge to locate them, even with a clear signal. He pointed towards the distant peak of Salpeterkop. 'A couple of weeks ago we had to climb halfway up that to find Angela.' Angela is an adult female and has a male cub.

After an hour, Richard picked up a signal and got a bearing. 'It's Mabula,' he said. The senior cat of the park, a male, almost 10 years old. We all got down. Richard carried the scanner but did not use it, trusting his experience to find the animal, knowing the sort of place he'd like to sit.

We walked through knee-high wire grass in flat terrain. Shades of browns, greens and yellows. If the animal was lying down in this, his camouflage would make him difficult to spot. But Richard was leading us directly to a solitary sweet thorn tree. 'Can you see him yet?' he asked me. I followed his line of sight. Nothing. It took another 50 metres before I could discern the cheetah, sitting in the shade, his gaze fixed on the black wildebeest in the middle distance. 'Reading the menu,' as Desh said.

Denis Costello

Having detected a signal, our group sets off in search of cheetah.

I thought we would stop, but we kept walking closer and closer. The collared animals have become accustomed to humans and are not alarmed by them. Mabula finally turned to look at us, his expression saying nothing. We stopped 20 metres away, and I was able to see what a magnificently beautiful animal he is, looking in perfect health, at the peak of his powers. He licked his lips and turned back to regard his domain.

For 15 wonderful minutes, we just stood and admired. I was happy to see that our presence caused the animal no distress. A couple of times he snapped his head forward towards the wildebeest, as if he might go to hunt. Desh warned us not to crouch down, as that would make us look like prey. I asked about the effect of the lions' reintroduction to the park, and if the cheetahs' behaviour has changed. He told me that they don't stay so long at a kill, eating the entrails and leaving the rest for lions and others to feed on. Also, they are less active at night, which is when they are in most danger from hunting lions. Overall, lions are responsible for just over 33 per cent of cheetah deaths in the EWT project reserves. Angela's cubs from last year have not been seen for some time.

Denis Costello

Richard explains how the tracking technology works.

Later I checked in with EWT Metapopulation Project coordinator Vincent van der Merwe. He told me that the project has been a great success, with cheetah numbers growing from 217 to the present 357 animals. 'In order to ensure long-term demographic and genetic health, we manage the population through relocations when necessary,' he said. Mountain Zebra National Park has played a big role in the battle to save the cheetah, and the Metapopulation Project now manages the cats in 57 reserves around South Africa. How wonderful it would be to see them reintroduced to my 'local' park, Hlane Royal in the Kingdom of eSwatini. **HM**

Shamwari

Rhinos in Shamwari are usually relaxed in the presence of walkers.

Addo Elephant National Park, the largest park in the Eastern Cape, doesn't offer walks in big game areas, although there are self-guided walks available in sections of the park that don't have dangerous game. The good news is that there is a big game reserve in the area that does cater for walking safaris: Shamwari Private Game Reserve, 7,000 hectares of protected habitat just an hour's drive north-east of Port Elizabeth.

Shamwari is 230 metres above sea level and has a diverse vegetation, with five of South Africa's eight biomes present. The dominant habitat is Albany thicket, with its distinctive spekboom and spikethorn trees. This supports kudu and other antelope species and small numbers of elephant, giraffe, buffalo, and white and black rhino. Lion, cheetah and leopard can be spotted. As well as being a driving and walking safari destination, the reserve is deeply involved in wildlife rehabilitation, operating big cat rescue facilities in partnership with the Born Free Foundation. The reserve also runs a volunteer programme, the Shamwari Conservation Experience. Day visits and self-driving are not allowed.

WALKING IN SHAMWARI PRIVATE GAME RESERVE

The Eastern Cape has good daytime temperatures for walking throughout the year, but winter nights are cold, below 10°C. September, October and November are excellent months, with the spring flowering bringing colour to the veld. December and January are the wettest months; the Eastern Cape has more rainfall than the Western Cape.

Shamwari Reserve has six luxury lodges where walking activities are available on request. In addition, the Explorer Camp is dedicated to walking safaris and operates in the summer months, from October to April.

Explorer Camp

■ Walk type	Wilderness trail
■ Booking	www.shamwari.com
■ Cost category	R3,000–R6,000
■ Group size	2–6
■ Min. age	16
■ Season	October–April

Shamwari

Shamwari reserve's two male cheetah are long-time residents.

Guests at Shamwari's Explorer Camp stay for two nights: Tuesday and Wednesday, or Friday and Saturday, with an optional third night (Sunday) on request. The camp has a minimal fence for safety and is beautifully situated, with a wooden deck overlooking the bushveld.

A game-viewing vehicle stays at the camp, so walkers can explore a different area each day. Walks are usually around four hours long, and participants over 65 should bring a medical certificate of fitness. The best close sightings of big animals are usually from the vehicle, and the walks focus on learning about the entire ecosystem of the reserve, from geology and soils to its varied flora, invertebrates and birdlife.

The deck at the Explorer Camp is the perfect spot for sundowners.

Shamwari

18 ■ KWANDWE PRIVATE GAME RESERVE

Kwandwe

The Great Fish River cuts a verdant path through Kwandwe Private Game Reserve.

In the heart of the Eastern Cape, the meandering Great Fish River is the central geographic feature of Kwandwe Private Game Reserve, its waters feeding 30 kilometres of riverine forest and a broad floodplain.

Kwandwe was established in 2001 through the amalgamation of nine farms, and expanded in 2005 with the addition of other farms. It boasts one of the highest land area-to-guest ratios in South Africa – 22,000 hectares for a maximum of just 60 guests, who can choose from two luxury lodges, a handful of private villas and a tented camp. The reserve is close to the attractive university town of Makhanda (Grahamstown), and about two hours' drive north-east of Port Elizabeth. Self-drives are not possible, but drives led by a Kwandwe guide and a tracker are available to day visitors. The reserve partners with a social development foundation to support local communities, and offers guests the chance to volunteer time or make donations.

Greater kudu and bushbuck have always been present, and the ongoing process of habitat restoration has seen the reintroduction of big game including giraffe, elephant, hippo, black and white rhino, and brown hyena. Cats present include cheetah, serval, African wildcat and small-spotted cat, and since returning in 2001, the lion population has grown to the point that some animals have been moved to repopulate other Eastern Cape reserves. The subtropical thicket vegetation is dominated by various types of euphorbia, with riverine thicket along the drainage lines.

Visitors to Kwandwe can set out to track black and white rhino on foot year-round.

WALKING IN KWANDWE PRIVATE GAME RESERVE

Kwandwe Private Game Reserve lies at an altitude of 250–490 metres above sea level and the area has hot and sometimes wet summers. Winter days are generally very pleasant and in the low 20s Celsius, but nights are chilly. Walking can be enjoyed at any time of year, with September to November the top months. The area is malaria-free.

As well as enjoying vehicle safaris, guests are encouraged to explore on foot and the floodplain of the Great Fish River makes for attractive and easy walking terrain. Kwandwe offers a range of options, from short guided nature interpretation walks (suitable for children aged 12 and over) to walking safaris instead of dawn game drives, spending three to four hours following animal trails. This option is best enjoyed at the Galpin Tented Camp, a recent addition to the reserve.

Galpin Tented Camp

Located in the remote southern corner of this expansive reserve, Galpin Tented Camp is a comfortable all-inclusive facility, designed for sole-use group bookings. The camp, named after the dam visible in the distance to the east, is unfenced, apart from a low barrier of sneezewood poles around the boma.

There are four tents, each with a view of the waterhole, which attracts buffalo, black rhino, elephant and, occasionally, big cats. Galpin Dam is a pleasant spot for fishing or for combining sundowners and wildlife spotting.

The isolated location of the camp is ideal for walks. After dinner, guides and guests discuss their plans for the next morning, including the starting time and duration of the walk. A game-viewing vehicle is at hand, allowing for flexibility in varying the starting points.

▩ Walk type	Day walk
▩ Booking	www.kwandwe.com
▩ Cost category	R3,000–R6,000
▩ Group size	1–8
▩ Min. age	16
▩ Season	January–December

eSwatini Tourism Authority

Mkhaya Game Reserve is a small lowveld park with grassveld, thickets and semi-deciduous forests that provide an ideal habitat for white rhino and other mammal species.

The Kingdom of eSwatini provides an attractive route – and another stamp for the passport – when travelling between the reserves of KwaZulu-Natal and the Kruger National Park. No visa is required for South Africans and for others who hold a passport that grants visa-free access to South Africa. The kingdom has several protected areas suited to walking, and two of these have big game: Hlane Royal National Park and Mkhaya Game Reserve.

In the kingdom's eastern lowveld, not far from Mozambique, Hlane Royal National Park is 22,000 hectares in size – about the same size as Phinda Private Game Reserve in KwaZulu-Natal (see chapter 2). It is 'royal' because it is held in trust for the nation by the king, His Majesty King Mswati III. Once a royal hunting ground, it became a national park in 1967 and is now the kingdom's flagship site of habitat protection, and home to eSwatini's only lions. The name of the main camp in the park, Ndlovu, is a clue as to what else to expect: *ndlovu* is the SiSwati word for elephant. A rustic camp, Ndlovu has no electricity, and evenings are spent by lamplight. It is located beside a large waterhole where white rhino wallow.

An hour's drive south of Hlane, the other big game park in the kingdom is the compact 10,000-hectare Mkhaya Game Reserve, known for its population of black and white rhino. There is just one permanent camp in this reserve, Stone Camp, which has attractive chalets that are completely open to the surrounding bushveld.

WALKING IN ESWATINI RESERVES

Weather conditions in eastern eSwatini are similar to the South African lowveld, with walking less attractive in summer when there is extreme humidity and the vegetation is dense. The months from June to September are mostly dry, with daytime temperatures in the mid-20s Celsius, and this is the best season for getting around on foot. The lowveld of eSwatini is a year-round malaria risk zone.

Hlane Royal National Park provides the best bushwalking options, with walks for day visitors and overnight guided hiking. It also allows for self-drive and self-catering, while Mkhaya Game Reserve is restricted to all-inclusive visits. In Mkhaya, overnight walks to a fly camp have been operated in the past, but at the time of writing only day walks were offered.

Between summer showers, Lucky Vilakati guides in Hlane Royal National Park.

Hlane Royal National Park day walks

Day walks operate year-round, leaving from Ndlovu Camp at 08:00 and 15:00. They take place in areas fenced off from dangerous game, and are led by a single unarmed guide. The walks last about two hours, and guests can request a focus on birding. It's also possible to ask for a walk that circles the largest dam in the park, Mahlindza, a locus for insects, antelopes and birds.

Walk type	Day walk
Booking	www.biggameparks.org
Cost category	Under R1,500
Group size	2–10
Min. age	13
Season	January–December

Hlane Royal National Park Ehlatsini Bush Trails

In addition to day walks, Big Game Parks also offers fully catered overnight bush walks in Hlane Royal National Park. The Ehlatsini Bush Trails experience involves a choice of one or two nights at the rustic Sundwini Fly Camp. Canvas bedrolls with mattresses are supplied and laid out on ground sheets under open gazebos. Trails depart from and return to Ndlovu Camp.

Walk type	Wilderness trail
Booking	www.biggameparks.org
Cost category	Under R1,500
Group size	4–10
Min. age	13
Season	April–September

There are four to six hours of walking each day following 4×4 and animal tracks through bushveld with pockets of dense thicket, riverine forest and stunning areas of open knob thorn veld. The game that can be seen includes rhino, giraffe, zebra, wildebeest, kudu and nyala. Overnight trails at Hlane are offered from 1 April to 30 September.

Mkhaya Game Reserve day walks

With just a single camp and low visitor numbers, Mkhaya Game Reserve is a tranquil reserve that tailors walks to visitors' requests. Short dawn walks from Stone Camp to a nearby bird hide are an option, and on game drives it is not unusual to get down from the vehicle to track animals on foot.

By request, longer outings of four to six hours can be arranged and for these, a packed lunch and water are supplied. If there are more than six participants, two guides are used. The bush is dense in Mkhaya and walkers need to be alert for unexpected close encounters with rhino, elephant and buffalo. There are no lions. Giraffe, sable antelope and tsessebe can also be spotted, and the reserve is high on the wish list of birdwatchers.

■ Walk type	Day walk
■ Booking	www.biggameparks.org
■ Cost category	Under R1,500
■ Group size	4–12
■ Min. age	13
■ Season	January–December

A group of women practise traditional Swati dancing steps at Mkhaya Game Reserve.

Sabie Botha

eSwatini's wildest corner

Just after sunset, I drove into Hlane Royal National Park's Ndlovu Camp and found the waterhole brimming: yes, the summer rains had been good. With no electricity for air conditioning, I cooled down after dark, sitting outside by the light of an oil lantern. The breeze delivered reminders that the wildness dial was turned up to 10. Odd noises, then the unmistakable roar of lion in the middle distance. Again, the strange noises, and heavy footsteps. I pointed my torch into the night, to find an elephant facing me – behind a sturdy fence.

In the morning, my memory fresh with lion sounds, I met my guide, Lucky Vilakati, and looked nervously at the stick he carried in place of a gun. He explained that Hlane has been fenced to keep the endangered species separate from us walkers. What followed was a crash course in nature education. Hlane may be smaller than more famous parks (I'm looking at you, Kruger), but it packs in a wealth of natural history.

We lolled in the shade of an acacia tree as Lucky told us of the uses for its wood, which include railway sleepers and mine shaft supports. Nearby, a giraffe delicately selected some leaves using its 15-centimetre tongue. Acacias can sense the giraffe feeding, and excrete a defensive foul-tasting chemical; they even communicate by means of a gas to other trees nearby to warn them.

A sudden flutter and a couple of 'wows' announced the appearance of a purple-crested turaco, the national bird of eSwatini. I've seen this beauty before, a crazy riot of rainbow feathers, but never tire of spotting another. As cameras snapped, we had a chat about how in the avian world it's the males who make the most effort to look beautiful.

Lucky fed our curiosity, bringing us to an aardvark excavation. He calls the aardvark the bushland 'minister for housing', as other animals – including pythons and warthogs – are happy to take over these burrows. We moved on animal trails and 4×4 tracks, pausing often in the shade to absorb more lore. Under a tamboti, Lucky described how its hardwood is preferred for furniture, and its powdered bark can cure headaches; yet if burned, the smoke can give you not only a headache but an upset stomach, too.

In the afternoon sun, I was happy to take a break from the trails and jump in a vehicle to enter the inner fenced park. The highlight was a very close encounter with three handsome lions – I swear I could smell their breath when they yawned! **HM**

Sabie Botha

Lucky Vilakati is an expert bird spotter.

20 ■ BOTSWANA

Karin Braby Photography/Mashatu Game Reserve

Mashatu Reserve's rugged sandstone landscape guarantees interesting walking experiences.

Visitors to the parks in the northern parts of South Africa should consider travelling a little further to Mashatu Game Reserve in neighbouring Botswana. The 29,000-hectare privately owned game reserve lies within the Northern Tuli Game Reserve in the south-eastern corner of Botswana. It is accessed via the Pont Drift border crossing, about six hours drive from Gauteng.

The name Mashatu refers to the endemic nyala berry trees, groves of which are found winding along the banks of the Majale and Limpopo rivers. Mashatu Game Reserve has diverse vegetation and landscapes, from undulating mopane veld and wide-open plains to riverine thickets and craggy sandstone hills. The reserve is known for some of the best predator viewing in Botswana, with near daily sightings of lion, leopard and cheetah, as well as hyena, black-backed jackal and the African wildcat. It's one of the few places where there's a chance to see the rare brown hyena. There's a full range of plains game, including giraffe, eland, zebra, the largest herds of elephant on private land in Africa, and about 350 different species of birds.

WALKING IN MASHATU GAME RESERVE

For most of the year Mashatu is extremely dry, with only summer thunderstorms bringing relief. The best walking season is from March to September, with April being a top month. From May onwards winter nights can be on the chilly side, and the landscape fades from green to brown until the next set of rains.

There are a small number of walking options in the reserve. Bush skills company EcoTraining (see chapter 5) operates a seasonal camp in Mashatu, which is the base for trail guide training, and also for fascinating multi-week courses for nature lovers. In the cooler months, WalkMashatu offers overnight trails.

Guests at Mashatu Lodge or Mashatu Tent Camp can take part in half-day walks at any time of year, although from November to the end of February long walks are discouraged. It's still feasible to head out before sunrise and be back at the camp before the heat sets in. The walks are gentle, and children from 12 years old can participate with a parent or guardian. Tracking of dangerous game is avoided if under-16s are present.

WalkMashatu Walking Safaris

■ Walk type	Wilderness trail
■ Booking	www.mashatu.com
■ Cost category	Over R6,000
■ Group size	2–8
■ Min. age	12
■ Season	March–October

Angelica Mills

Guide Stuart Quinn and walkers stop to admire the view on their early morning outing.

WalkMashatu operates three- and four-night walking safaris that explore the western part of the reserve and the Motloutse River area. The sandstone outcrops are similar to those in the Mapungubwe National Park, and make for dramatic photogenic terrain. A popular destination is the Mmamagwa Ruins complex, which is of the same historical period as the ruins at Mapungubwe.

Walkers overnight at a choice of three wild camps. One of these, Mohave Camp, is a permanent camp used only for walking trails. At the Kgotla Camp, guests sleep on camp beds around a central fire, protected in a traditionally constructed leadwood log boma. This camp is only used when there is little risk of rain from April to October. It has the essential comforts, including flush toilets and hot showers. A third camp, Serolo Safari Camp, is on the floodplain of the Limpopo River.

A typical three-night trail sees walkers exploring the Motloutse River area on the first day, covering up to eight kilometres. The second and third days could cover over 20 kilometres each, visiting the Mmamagwa Ruins, tracking elephants, seeking out the dens of brown hyena and learning tracking skills. On the last day, the group walks 10–13 kilometres, staying close to the Limpopo River, before returning to the Serolo Camp and departure following showers and brunch.

BIBLIOGRAPHY

Bryden, Bruce. *A Game Ranger Remembers*. Johannesburg: Jonathan Ball, 2009.

Carnaby, Trevor. *Beat about the Bush: Mammals and Birds*. Johannesburg: Jacana Media, 2014.

Carruthers, Vincent. *The Wildlife of Southern Africa – A Field Guide to the Animals and Plants of the Region*. Cape Town: Struik Nature, 2018.

Emmett, Megan and Pattrick, Sean. *Game Ranger in Your Backpack: All-in-One Interpretive Guide to the Lowveld*. Pretoria: Briza, 2012.

Estes, Richard Despard. *The Behaviour Guide to African Mammals*. Berkeley: University of California Press, 2012.

Gordon, Jeff. *101 Kruger Tales: Extraordinary Stories from Ordinary Visitors to the Kruger National Park*. Cape Town: Struik Nature, 2015.

Gutteridge, Lee and Liebenberg, Louis. *Mammals of Southern Africa and their Tracks and Signs*. Johannesburg: Jacana Media, 2013.

Joubert, Salomon. *The Kruger National Park: A History* (3 volumes). Bryanston: High Branching, 2007.

Liebenberg, Louis. *A Photographic Guide to Tracks and Tracking in Southern Africa*. Cape Town: Struik Nature, 2008.

Linscott, Graham. *Into the River of Life: A Biography of Ian Player*. Johannesburg: Jonathan Ball, 2013.

Player, Ian. *The White Rhino Saga*. New York: Stein and Day, 1973.

Player, Ian. *Zululand Wilderness: Shadow and Soul*. Cape Town: David Philip, 1998.

Sinclair, Ian; Hockey, Phil; Tarboton, Warwick; Perrins, Niall; Rollinson, Dominic and Ryan, Peter. *Sasol Birds of Southern Africa* (5th Revised Edition). Cape Town: Struik Nature, 2020.

Steele, Nick. *Game Ranger on Horseback*. Cape Town: Books of Africa, 1968.

Stuart, Chris and Stuart, Mathilde. *Stuarts' Field Guide to the Tracks and Signs of Southern, Central and East African Wildlife*. Cape Town: Struik Nature, 2019.

Van den Heever, Alex; Mhlongo, Renias and Benadie, Karel. *Tracker Manual: A Practical Guide to Animal Tracking in Southern Africa*. Cape Town: Struik Nature, 2017.

Van Wyk, Braam and Van Wyk, Piet. *Field Guide to Trees of Southern Africa*. Cape Town: Struik Nature, 2018.

USEFUL WEBSITES

- **www.fgasa.co.za** Field Guides Association of Southern Africa, the main industry body for professional guides.
- **www.peaceparks.org** Peace Parks Foundation; contains information about Transfrontier Conservation Areas, including the Great Limpopo Transfrontier Conservation Area and the Great Mapungubwe Transfrontier Conservation Area.
- **www.sanparks.org/forums** A forum where SANParks visitors can meet and chat, ask questions, and read news and announcements from SANParks.
- **www.inaturalist.org** A citizen science site where amateur and professional naturalists can post images and other details of their encounters with flora and fauna.
- **www.africawild-forum.com** A forum for information about and discussion of conservation issues.

OPERATOR CONTACT INFORMATION

Below are the websites and contact details of the walk operators, arranged by national park or game reserve. The relevant page numbers are supplied for quick reference.

HLUHLUWE-IMFOLOZI PARK (P. 50)

Ezemvelo KZN Wildlife
Website: www.kznwildlife.com
Email: bookings@kznwildlife.com (Central reservations); trails@kznwildlife.com (Wilderness trail bookings)
Tel: +27 (0) 33 845 1000 (Central reservations)
Tel: +27 (0) 33 845 1067 (Wilderness trails)

Wilderness Leadership School (pp. 62)
Website: www.wildernesstrails.org.za
Email: reservations@wildernesstrails.org.za
Tel: +27 (0) 83 225 5960

Rhino Ridge Safari Lodge (p. 63)
Website: www.rhinoridge.co.za
Email: res@isibindi.co.za
Tel: +27 (0) 35 474 1473

PHINDA PRIVATE GAME RESERVE (PP. 68)

Website: www.andbeyond.com
Email: webenquiries@andBeyond.com
Tel: +27 (0) 11 809 4300

UMKHUZE GAME RESERVE (PP. 70)

Ezemvelo KZN Wildlife
Website: www.kznwildlife.com
Email: bookings@kznwildlife.com
Tel: +27 (0) 35 573 9004

ITHALA GAME RESERVE (P. 72)

Ezemvelo KZN Wildlife
Website: www.kznwildlife.com
Email: bookings@kznwildlife.com
Tel: +27 (0) 34 983 2540

KRUGER NATIONAL PARK (PP. 74)

SANParks
Day walks from rest camps (p. 80)
Website: www.sanparks.org
Email: reservations@sanparks.org
Tel: + 27 (0) 12 428 9111 (Central reservations)

Day walks from bushveld camps (p. 80)
Bateleur Bushveld Camp: +27 (0) 13 735 6843
Biyamiti Bushveld Camp: +27 (0) 13 735 6171
Shimuwini Bushveld Camp: +27 (0) 13 735 6683
Shingwedzi Bushveld Camp: +27 (0) 13 735 6806/7
Sirheni Bushveld Camp: +27 (0) 13 735 6860
Talamati Bushveld Camp: +27 (0) 13 735 6343

Day walks from gates (p. 81)
Crocodile Bridge Gate: +27 (0) 13 735 6012
Malelane Gate: +27 (0) 13 735 6152
Numbi Gate: +27 (0) 13 735 5133; Cell +27 (0) 64 750 2318
Orpen Gate: +27 (0) 13 735 6355 or +27 (0) 735 5127
Paul Kruger Gate: +27 (0) 13 735 5107; Cell +27 (0) 64 750 2321
Phabeni Gate: +27(0) 13 735 5890; Cell +27 (0) 64 750 2322

KRUGER NATIONAL PARK (cont.)

Phalaborwa Gate: +27 (0) 13 735 3547
Punda Maria Gate: +27 (0) 13 735 6873

Wilderness and backpacking trails (pp. 84–104)
Website: www.sanparks.org
Email: specialisedreservations@sanparks.org
Tel: +27 (0) 12 426 5111

SANParks Honorary Rangers (pp. 105)
Bush camps (pp. 106–107)
Website: www.sanparksvolunteers.org
Email: bushcamps@honoraryrangers.org

The Kruger Trail (p. 108)
Website: www.thekrugertrail.com
Email: thekrugertrail@gmail.com

Rhino Walking Safaris (pp. 109)
Website: www.rws.co.za
Email: info@seoloafrica.com
Tel: +27 (0) 11 467 1886

Singita Sweni Lodge (pp. 110)
Website: www.singita.com
Email: enquiries@singita.com
Tel: +27 (0) 21 683 3424

Jock Safari Lodge (p. 111)
Website: www.jocksafarilodge.com
Email: reservations@jocksafarilodge.com
Tel: +27 (0) 13 010 0019

RETURNAfrica (p. 112)
Website: www.returnafrica.com
Email: reservations@returnafrica.com
Tel: +27 (0) 11 646 1391

African-Born Safaris (pp. 120–121)
Website: www.africanbornsafaris.com
Email: info@africanbornsafaris.com
Tel: +27 (0) 21 813 5950

MANYELETI PRIVATE NATURE RESERVE (P. 124)

Pungwe Safari Camp (p. 125)
Website: www.pungwe.co.za
Email: info@pungwe.co.za
Tel: +27 (0) 82 853 9533

TIMBAVATI PRIVATE NATURE RESERVE (P. 126)

Bateleur Safari Camp (p. 127)
Website: www.bateleursafaricamp.com
Email: reservations@bateleursafaricamp.com
Tel: +27 (0) 21 683 0234

Tanda Tula Field Camp (p. 128)
Website: www.tandatula.com
Email: reservations@tandatula.com
Tel: + 27 (0) 15 793 3191

TIMBAVATI PRIVATE NATURE RESERVE (cont.)

Simbavati Trails Camp (p. 129)
Website: www.simbavati.com
Email: info@simbavati.com
Tel: +27 (0) 87 151 4520

Lowveld Trails Company (p. 130)
Website: www.lowveldtrails.co.za
Email: admin@lowveldtrails.co.za

KLASERIE PRIVATE NATURE RESERVE (P. 132)

Africa on Foot (p. 133)
Websites: www.africaonfoot.com;
www.wilderness-trails.co.za (Wilderness trail)
Email: reservations@sundestinations.co.za
Tel: +27 (0) 21 712 5284

Klaserie Sands Safari Trails (p. 135)
Website: www.klaseriesands-safaritrails.com
Email: reservations@klaseriesands.com
Tel: +27 (0) 15 817 1800

LETABA RANCH NATURE RESERVE (P. 136)

Mtomeni Safari Camp (p. 137)
Website: www.africanivoryroute.co.za
Email: info@africanivoryroute.co.za
Tel: +27 (0) 15 781 0690 or +27 (0) 15 781 0343

Spirited Adventures (p. 141)
Website: www.spiritedadventures.co.za
Email: enquiries@spiritedadventures.co.za
Tel: +27 (0) 82 777 5590

MAPUNGUBWE NATIONAL PARK (P. 142)

SANParks
Website: www.sanparks.org
Email: mapungubwe@sanparks.org
Tel: +27 (0) 15 534 7923/24

MARAKELE NATIONAL PARK (PP. 146)

SANParks
Website: www.sanparks.org
Email: marakele@sanparks.org
Tel: +27 (0) 14 777 6928/29/30/31

SANParks Honorary Rangers (p. 150)
Bush camps (p. 150)
Website: www.sanparksvolunteers.org
Email: bushcamps@honoraryrangers.org

Marataba Trails (p. 151)
Website: www.marataba.co.za
Email: concierge@more.co.za
Tel: +27 (0) 10 109 4900

PILANESBERG GAME RESERVE (P. 152)

Mankwe Game Trackers (p. 152)
Website: www.mankwegametrackers.co.za
Email: suncity@mankwegametrackers.co.za
Tel: +27 (0) 14 552 5020 or +27 (0) 14 557 3530

PILANESBERG GAME RESERVE (cont)

Legacy Hotels (p. 153)
Website: www.legacyhotels.co.za
Email: bakgame@legacyhotels.co.za
Tel: +27 (0) 14 552 6226

KGALAGADI TRANSFRONTIER PARK (P. 154)

SANParks
Website: www.sanparks.org
Email: kgalagadi@sanparks.org
Tel: + 27 (0) 54 561 2000 (Twee Rivieren)

!Xaus Lodge (p. 155)
Website: www.xauslodge.co.za
Email: info@xauslodge.co.za
Tel: +27 (0) 21 701 7860

SANBONA WILDLIFE RESERVE (P. 160)

Website: www.sanbona.com
Email: reservations@sanbona.com
Tel: +27 (0) 21 010 0028

GONDWANA GAME RESERVE (P. 162)

Website: www.gondwanagr.co.za
Email: reservations@gondwanagr.co.za
Tel: +27 (0) 21 555 0807

MOUNTAIN ZEBRA NATIONAL PARK (P. 166)

SANParks
Website: www.sanparks.org
Email: mountainzebra@sanparks.org
Tel: +27 (0) 48 801 5700/1

SHAMWARI PRIVATE GAME RESERVE (P. 172)

Website: www.shamwari.com
Email: reservations@shamwari.com
Tel: +27 (0) 42 203 1111

KWANDWE PRIVATE GAME RESERVE (P. 174)

Website: www.kwandwe.com
Email: reservations@kwandwe.co.za
Tel: +27 (0) 46 622 7897

THE KINGDOM OF ESWATINI (P. 176)

**Hlane Royal National Park (p. 177) and
Mkhaya Game Reserve (p. 178)**
Website: www.biggameparks.org
Email: reservations@biggameparks.org
Tel: +268 (25) 28 3943/4

BOTSWANA (P. 180)

Mashatu Game Reserve (pp. 180)
WalkMashatu (p. 181)
Website: www.mashatu.com
Email: reservations@mashatu.com
Tel: +27 (0) 31 761 3440